al·pha·bet·i·ca

An A–Z Creativity Guide for Collage and Book Artists

GLOUCESTER MASSACHUSETTS

QUARRY BOOKS

LYNNE PERRELLA

First published in the United States of America by
Quarry Books, a member of
Quayside Publishing Group
33 Commercial Street
Gloucester, Massachusetts 01930-5089
Tel: (978) 282-9590
Fax: (978) 283-2742
www.rockpub.com

Library of Congress Cataloging-in-Publication Data
Perrella, Lynne.
  Alphabetica : an A–Z creativity guide for collage and book artists / Lynne Perrella.
    p.   cm.
  ISBN 1-59253-176-8 (pbk.)
  1. Handicraft. 2. Paper work. 3. Collage. I. Title.
TT157.P385 2005
702'.81'2—dc22   2005013009
                                                                          CIP

ISBN 1-59253-176-8

10 9 8 7 6 5 4 3

Design: Laura H. Couallier, Laura Herrmann Design
Photography: Allan Penn Photography

Printed in Singapore

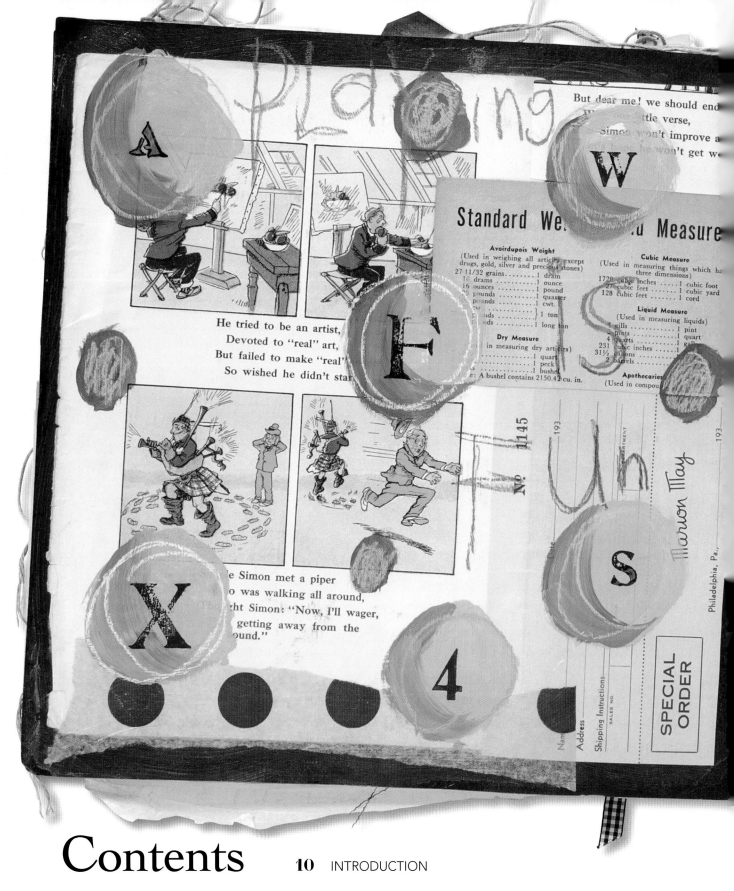

Contents

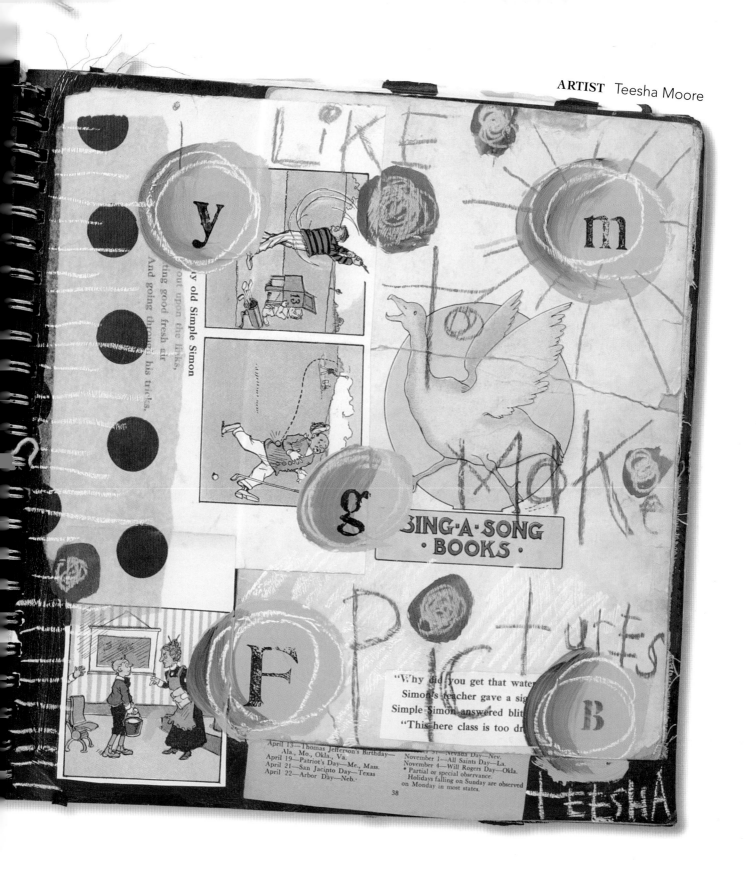

Introduction

Key to Alphabetica Grid
(see pages 8, 9, and 11)

A is for Altered
B is for Brown Bag
C is for Crackle
D is for Drips
E is for Envelope
F is for Feathers
G is for Gesso
H is for Hinges
I is for Ink
J is for Junk
K is for Knots
L is for Letters
M is for Music
N is for Nature
O is for Openings
P is for Positive/Negative
Q is for Quotations
R is for Rubber
S is for Stencil
T is for Transparencies
U is for Umber
V is for Vellum
W is for Wax
X is for Xerox
Y is for Yarn
Z is for Zigzag
0–9 is for Found Objects

A child plays with a set of alphabet blocks. Too young to read the letters or grasp their meaning, she is captivated by the chunky, friendly shape in her hand. The not-yet-discovered significance of the letter "A" or the cheerful image of an apple does not prevent her from using the blocks to create a secret world of discovery and experimentation.

"C" is for Child's play. If we keep in mind that creating art is always a blend of work and play, we can return to the foundation of learning and discovery: the alphabet. And let's not forget numbers! Part of growing up and cracking the code of knowledge is learning our alphabet, knowing how to count to ten, and eventually learning the amplified joys of reading, rhyming, writing, adding, and subtracting. With letters and numbers in our hip pocket, we hold all the keys to the kingdom.

As this book shows, the most engaging and provocative ideas are usually deceptively simple. What would happen if a group of fourteen artists collaborated on a project based on the alphabet and numbers? This book documents much of what happened as a result of that collaboration. Each artist began by creating a journal that would travel the country and be added to by thirteen other artists. The focus: letters and numbers. In the spirit of childlike experimentation, the journals took on other forms of expression: a long, accordion-fold screen; a red plaid children's lunchbox; a cigar box wrapped in stylish papers with a beaded closure. Several purchased journals were transformed by unique cover embellishments, including an antique Scrabble game with moveable letters and a chalkboard for "leaving a message" for the next artist. Another spiral-bound book was completely tiled in handsome brass letter stencils.

Some artists were reminded of youthful rope-skipping rhymes, while others explored ancient, arcane semaphores, ciphers, and symbols. The beauty and history of letterforms were investigated, decoded, and celebrated. Everything was fair game. After all, "E" is for Experiment!

As you explore these pages, you will meet the artists, see their work, and learn their favorite methods for working and playing. You will also gain insight into artistic collaborations, materials, and creativity. Get ready to enjoy a creative journey, A to Z. (And let's not forget the numbers!)

—*Lynne Perrella*

1

Books
and More:
Exploring
Forms

The above quote was irresistible, not only because it defines a lifelong love of books, but because it holds the key to the *Alphabetica* artist's collaboration. It contains some apt words and phrases: enter…surprise …truths…see imaginatively into someone else's life. As these collaborative journals traveled the country, they became the ambassadors for the artists, some of whom have never actually met. The books created anticipation, and invited the recipient to engage, play, and experiment.

The artists selected the themes of the alphabet and numerals because it was openended and would provide fascinating common ground. Fourteen artists—all lovers of words, lyrics, symbols, and signs—each created a journal that traveled the country for more than a year, collecting entries from all the other participants.

Whether constructed with great care using time-honored techniques, or invented from seat-of-the-pants improvisation, the various books opened their covers to everything and anything. Elongated books were made even longer by fold-outs and additions. Fabric entries were stitched, stapled, and glued alongside paper, cardboard, and painted pages. Three-dimensional objects were incorporated into the books with a sense of whimsy and inventiveness. Treasured collectibles were attached to the pages, and sent along to new, appreciative owners. Visual puns were explored, and music was incorporated via custom CDs or by visual presentations of favorite song lyrics. One unfortunate journal was accidentally dunked in a mud puddle, but emerged better-than-ever with a new cover. Best of all, the artists used what they knew—or thought they knew—about each other to formulate their creative strategies. Eventually, all the books arrived back at their starting point, full of stories, ideas, and surprises. Take a look.

ARTIST
Lynne Perrella

Incoming!

The Journals of the
Alphabetica Collaboration

1. Lisa Renner
2. Lisa Hoffman
3. Linn C. Jacobs
4. Lesley Riley
5. Lesley Jacobs
6. Teesha Moore
7. Claudine Hellmuth
8. Monica Riffe
9. Michelle Ward
10. Lynne Perrella
11. Karen Michel
12. Shirley Ende-Saxe
13. Sarah Fishburn
14. Judi Riesch

P is for plaid,

and pack a lunch. Going along with the "no rules" invitation to participate in this collaboration, the artist lured the other participants into a game of Fill the Lunchbox. The cheerful vintage lunchbox traveled the country, evoking memories of grade-school spelling bees, rope-skipping rhymes, and girlhood birthday parties. When the lunchbox finally returned, it was filled to the top with light-hearted and richly colored artwork, including some offbeat submissions. A long fold-out booklet in candy colors was designed to hold a CD of retro tunes, and a funky purple diary with a lock and a tiny key was tucked inside the box. Proving that color can be the springboard for ideas, another artist raided her stash of fabrics and sewing notions to create the vibrant red entry shown at the bottom right.

ARTIST
Sarah Fishburn

>

THIS LUNCHBOX BELON

S. ELYNN FISHBURN

MRS. BANKS
GRADE 4
JULIA KEEN
ELEMENTARY
TUCSON, ARIZ.
~1964

ARTIST
Lesley Riley

>

language arranged in an order fixed by custom
a b c d e f g h I j k l m n o p q r s t u v w x y z

ABC

...ey Shirl...

...e Li...de-S... Sa... Fishburn

...offi...

...el T...y JACOBS

...na Moore

...Reb... Riesch

...le Ward

...resenting a sound of
...nit of an alphabet. λ

ALPHABETICA

U is for unfolding

ARTIST
Linn C. Jacobs

and unity. Zen quiz: What is fifteen and a half feet long when opened, tied with black ribbon, and full of artwork? Answer: This unique, multipaneled "accordion-screen" book. This journal was a favorite among the participating artists, not only because it was such a surprising book form, but also because many of the participants enjoyed working off the bound-book page and then attaching their pages to the sturdy panels of the screen. The originating artist selected handsome Asian-themed papers to cover the book boards and provided an additional surprise by adding an entire alphabet of definitions to the back of each panel. (For example, "V is for Vivid.") The artists in the collaboration could use the words as prompts for their entries, or simply enjoy the pure serendipity of word versus image. Either way, this elegant unfolding book provides a perfect meeting ground for fourteen artists—giving new meaning to the phrase, "an unfolding drama."

"A 2 Z"

ARTIST
Shirley Ende-Saxe

>

The originating artist spotted the possibilities of a cardboard letter stencil as a collage element and affixed it to the cover of her journal. She also added metallic and acrylic paints, rub-on lettering, and abstract shapes punched from dictionary entries that she hand-colored with thick markers. The narrow shape of the journal led to many unique approaches as each artist decided whether to turn the book lengthwise or sideways. The prevailing desire to "just keep going" led to a variety of creative add-ons.

L is for long

ARTIST
Karen Michel

∧

and lean. When this narrow journal started making the rounds, the artists could not resist pushing its elongated proportions to the max with fold-out panels attached by spiral bindings, metal eyelets laced with wire, and suede insertions affixed with contact cement. This artist sprinkled the letters "A R T" throughout her entry, used extra-large transfers of dictionary definitions alongside a significant photo, and included a hand-written quote about anticipation. Although other disparate elements such as postage stamps and a glittered heart appear, the composition comes together through a strong use of color and a spirited theme of revelation.

during the
FULL MOON
I anticipate
lovely
flutters....

B is for book of dreams.

You'd hardly look twice at this modest-sized three-ring binder in a stationery store, and yet this artist saw its vast potential and used her love of color and surface design to transform it into something quite special. She primed the cover of the book with gesso, and used acrylic pigments to add deep, lush colors. Using gel medium, she transferred one of her own drawings to cotton fabric and used a set of alphabet letters to imprint a border. As the book traveled, it acquired the well-loved look that we see here. Each artist's submission lent a provocative peek at feathers, soft ribbons, touchable cotton yarn, metal tabs, and trailing thread ends.

ARTIST
Karen Michel

<

P is for patterned papers

ARTIST
Lesley Jacobs

>

and page pebbles. This artist looked through the empty packaging containers in her studio, and she came across the perfect elongated box to use for her journal. By covering the box inside and out in a multitude of colorful and patterned papers, she made the container her own. She found clear acrylic page pebbles at a scrapbook supply store and used the almost-impossible-to-break domes to highlight the word "alphabet." Buttons, bangles, and beads create a closure.

T is for torrid,

ARTIST
Shirley
Ende-Saxe

tropical colors. Drizzles of acrylic glazes; drips of paint; small, uneven swatches of cloth; urgent scribbles with a pastel chalk; papers cut out with pinking shears—all of these disparate elements have an unexpected harmony. Try this artist's fearless approach with multiple art supplies, and consider her guiding words: "Never underestimate the power of just making the art happen."

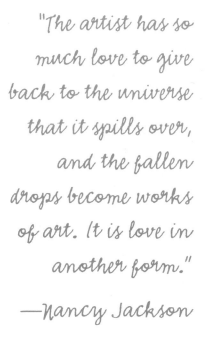

"The artist has so much love to give back to the universe that it spills over, and the fallen drops become works of art. It is love in another form."

—Nancy Jackson

ARTIST
Lisa Renner

The Telling Detail

The artist mounted a colorful clown portrait on foam core, and then used a wide range of offbeat materials to amplify the drama of the image. Elegant costume touches, such as black netting, a collar of bird feathers, beading, velvet, and metallic fabrics, all prove transformative.

ARTIST
Lisa Renner

The Telling Detail

A familiar face was transferred to rugged watercolor paper, and additional layers were added to form a collage. The layers, including a variety of unlikely images, such as golden joss paper, animal print tissue, and colorful florals, surround the classic portrait.

ARTIST
Judi Riesch

The Telling Detail

A timeless image of statuary was captured on film, and then further explored with a Polaroid transfer and additional mark-making using acrylic paints, stencils, and expressive drawing with Prismacolor pencils. This artist has been able to use and reuse her entire library of photographic images by implementing various transfer methods to create a wide variety of moods and themes.

ARTIST
Karen Michel

The Telling Detail

This drawing is an example of a recurring image that appears in various colors, textures, sizes, and renditions in the artist's work. In this instance, she rubbed multiple layers of water-soluble oil pastels into the surface to build up a richly colored painterly surface.

ARTIST
Judi Riesch

The Telling Detail

Examine the edge! Do you want your journal pages to announce themselves even when the book is still closed? This artist used sturdy metal tabs found at a stationery warehouse and inserted her own numerals and typography in colors that coordinated with her journal pages. The tabs make reference to the journal's origins as a conventional three-ring binder, while providing a tactile and sophisticated way to display numerals and letters outside the margin of the page.

ARTIST
Lynne Perrella

The Telling Detail

This artist found a vintage cardboard paper doll and gave it a rigorous scuffing with sandpaper to achieve a softened look. Articulated arms were attached with brads, and a length of black cord was strung with alphabet letters as a necklace.

ARTIST
Lesley Riley

The Telling Detail

These carefully gathered items suggest a child's collection of keepsakes: an old photograph, two bottle caps glued together to create a medallion, a length of ribbon, and a tiny pearl button. The portrait is achieved by transferring the image to rugged cotton fabric, and the uneven stitches around the edges create a heartfelt pattern.

ARTIST
Sarah Fishburn

The Telling Detail

The artist gave a row of hearts three-dimensional interest by inserting brass upholstery tacks into the center of each heart. The dreamy, muffled colors of the page surface are in contrast with the sharp transparency of archival images and alphabets.

 A is for antique

ARTIST
Lesley Riley

∧

spelling wheel. We've all experienced that moment when we see something we love, but have no earthly purpose for it, and no justification for buying it. Undeterred, we acquire it anyhow. This artist purchased an old spelling game in an online auction and spotted the perfect opportunity to use it as a cover embellishment when this alphabet-themed collaboration got started. After finding the perfect-sized journal, she raided the workshop to find construction-grade cement to affix the game and added a sturdy clip to hold a piece of white chalk. As each recipient unwrapped the journal, she would discover a message left by the previous artist. The playful hands-on nature of the vintage cover embellishment set the tone, and many of the artists chose to follow along with the nostalgic school-themed mood. Some of the artist's sign-in bookmarks appear at right. The end result was a book full of remembrances and strong narrative stories.

Artist credits (right)

Judi Riesch **1**
Lynne Perrella **2**
Lesley Riley **3**
Sarah Fishburn **4**
Michelle Ward **5**
Karen Michel **6**
Shirley Ende-Saxe **7**

1

2

3

4

5

6

7

 **M** is for make
it meaningful.

ARTIST
Lisa Hoffman

Can't tell a book by its cover? Not in this case. The artist wears her heart on her sleeve, and tells us of her love of a whole litany of things: found objects; her spirited white dog, Matisse; weathered planks of wood left out in the Colorado sun to bleach and weather to a fine patina. The divine and often-overlooked beauty of fabric flowers, imprinted tin, and a tiny dog license that offers a sly wink, provide apt embellishments for the hot pink journal. This book is yet another example of a three-ring binder; this time, one intended to be used as a photo scrapbook, but perfect as an art journal.

THE
ALPhA DOGS
FiNiSHiNG SCHOOL
FOR STRONG - BRAVE & RESOURCEFUL WOMEN

is for Clara.

ARTIST
Judi Riesch

"N" is for Nellie. "M" is for Mabel. And "G" is for Grace. Four young girls happily exchanged autograph books in the fall of 1897. Little did they know that their fond words to one another would re-emerge as the central element in an art journal more than a hundred years later. This artist also highlighted two of her special collections on these pages: the hushed colors of old fabric trimmings and edgings, and a vintage autograph book. Exercises from a classroom notebook may display perfect penmanship, but the charm of the autograph book prevails, with humorous misspellings and the round loopy handwriting of girls trying hard to be grown up.

Try This: Remember this book-within-a-book idea the next time you are considering using actual tactile elements on your pages. Consider vintage postcard fold-outs, Baedecker travel maps, astronomy charts, nautical graphs, and architectural blueprints. Even slightly dimensional elements, such as vintage baby spoons, gloves (in elegant satin or rugged leather), small beaded Asian coin purses, and tintypes in presentation cases, can be attached to pages, proving that there is nothing like adding "the real thing" to your artwork.

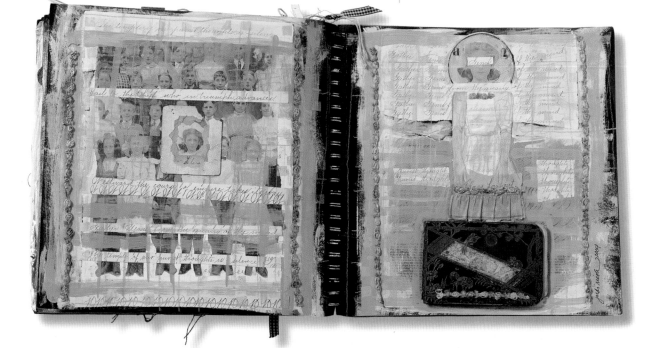

L is for the lure

ARTIST
Lesley Jacobs

of fishing. Fishermen are famous for their tall tales, but this artist from the American Northwest has lined up an impressive array of images to show her love of fishing. In her journal, we can count the cut-out fish in the barrel and explore a colorful listing of fish from "angel" to "zebra." Old encyclopedia entries show row upon row of shells, and other beachside flotsam provide a backdrop for her clever, well-constructed add-ons, including a booklet showing the artist as a young girl making her first catch. Take a closer look, and small details such as a plastic lure and brass flashers attached to the paper fish will convince you of this artist's love of the sport. The vintage beach beauties seem to agree. Notice how this artist has been able to take us for an intimate look at something she cares about, revealing her zeal through her journal pages.

Try This: Indoor and outdoor hobbyists, take note: altered books and journals are the perfect place to declare your interests and fascinations using innovative page layouts. Imagine an art journal with pages of rugged plastic or canvas depicting a watery kayak adventure, or a gardening scrapbook with a convincing square of forever-green Astroturf glued to the cover. For lovers of vintage clothing and costume details, thrift shops often have a rummage box full of tattered garments, trimmings, mismatched gloves, and odd buttons; these can be glued or stitched to pages for a tactile look.

The Right Stuff: Surfaces and Materials

2

> *"May the beauty we love,*
> *be what we do."* —Rumi

Whether you create collages, altered books, art journals, or scrapbook pages, here is some advice: Go maximal and textural! Nearly any object or material can be used to bring fresh, surprising, plentiful exuberance to your pages.

Throw out the rule book and acknowledge that anything that piques your interest can and should be part of your artwork. Whether you haunt estate sales and flea markets, or enjoy walks in the woods or at the beach, all your finds can be added to pages and covers. Part of the joy of collecting is realizing that there are infinite ways of including your finds into your artwork.

Consider the possibilities: tin, twigs, toothpicks, and twine; daguerreotypes and dog tags; brocade and brown grocery bags. Literally anything can be pinned, stapled, glued, stitched, grommeted, or lashed to a page or cover. This chapter will give you ideas for using those "I just had to have it" finds. You'll also get plenty of tips to enliven a well-loved collection.

Finding new ways of using what you love is what this chapter is all about. Come and browse through our finest collections, our strangest widgets, and our funniest dime-store treasures. You'll get plenty of ideas for turning your collections into perfect "Ta da!" touches. And, even better, you will be reminded that part of the fun of being an artist is using your eye to spot endless possibilities.

ARTIST
Lynne Perrella

"Improvisation can be either a last resort or an established way of evoking creativity."

—Mary Catherine Bateson

ARTIST
Teesha Moore

S is for stitching.

This artist gets extra mileage out of her own collaged and painted art journal pages by transferring the vibrant, personal pages to fabric. This gives her the opportunity to reuse the images in a new way, and machine stitching is a practical way of affixing the fabric collage elements while adding a new form of mark-making with rows of decorative sewing. She incorporates variety and whimsy into her stitched covers with the addition of decorative braid, ribbon, seam tape, metallic fabrics, touchable brocade patches, and tactile velvet ribbon.

T is for typography,

ARTIST
Judi Riesch

tintypes, and type trays. What would it feel like to enter an old print shop and slide open the narrow oak drawers of a typesetter's tall, well-worn cabinet? What would we find? Daguerreotypes, an old-type specimen book listing vintage fonts, cardboard letter slugs, or a worn photo mat with multiple openings? By creating a faux type drawer with fascinating paper enclosures and attachments, the artist provides a feeling of discovery as well as time travel. Her color choices suggest weathered, workmanlike surfaces. Touchable elements, such as soft ribbon ties and a moveable cardboard bookmark, encourage the viewer to play along with the game.

Try This: Dress patterns (and other forms of printed tissue paper) are ideal for adding layers to a collage or page. In this case, the artist has used torn strips of old patterns to introduce yet another form of lettering and typographic information, allowing the previous layers to show through. Using matte medium as your adhesive, try applying the tissue smoothly, or in a deliberately wrinkled or textured way, to create fascinating folds and creases.

C is for color,

class pictures, canvas, and collections. A memorable collection of vintage class photos was the starting point for this distinctive, multilayered page. Seven layers of fabric were stitched to a fabric background, along with an array of photo transfers on white canvas, floral prints, and plaids in back-to-school colors of yellow, orange, melon, and crimson. Lines of machine stitching, trailing thread ends, raveled selvages, and fringed fabrics lend a made-by-hand look to this heartfelt all-fabric page.

ARTIST
Lesley Riley
^

The Telling Detail

These touchable pages, with lift-up fabrics and fold-out details, invite exploration and interaction. The artist features an entire collection of themed photos, which increases the story-telling aspect of the journal entry and emphasizes the tactile nature of the varied, sturdy-to-silky fabrics. As the viewer lifts each fabric page and explores the next color and image, he or she enters the narrative world created by the artist.

G is for grid,

ARTIST
Monica Riffe

∨

and for gathering and graphics. Grid systems are a time-honored technique used by graphic designers to organize and present numerous elements on a page, while creating harmony and visual cohesion. The grid on this journal page tips its hat to that tradition, while presenting fascinating texture, rampant color, and surprising "discovered" collage elements that redefine the concept. None of these collected art supplies are precious or costly—and yet the finished page is a show-stopper of vivid colors and rescued wonders. The distorted background print was made by crumpling the morning newspaper and placing it on the copier. The ultra-colorful grid elements are swatches of dried paints peeled from an innovative palette: a plastic Frisbee! The final tactile touch was created with lines of machine stitching, which outline and define the rows of colorful paint chips. Black cotton thread ends provide additional texture to a page that begs to be touched.

Try This: Want the look of a newspaper without the distraction of clearly readable words or headlines? Crumple, fold, or crimp the paper before putting it on the copier. You can also put a sheet of tissue paper, semi-opaque vellum, or tracing paper over the newspaper, place it on the copier, and "shoot" through it for a mysterious look. Keep folding and unfolding the newspaper, creating a file of papers to be used in future collages. Don't forget that some of your newspaper-themed copies can be put through the copier with other line art to get a layered appearance. The real fun begins when you try unusual pairings, such as large-scale Japanese stencil designs photocopied onto a newspaper background. The possibilities are endless!

The Telling Detail

If chips of dried paint look this good, think of other possible ways of reclaiming discarded artwork. Seize the moment and go through the trash in your studio. Failed collages can be cut up into smaller sections and reassembled into a mosaic pattern by pressing the small pieces into modeling paste. Or try gluing the segments onto a journal cover for a tiled effect.

S is for signs,

ARTIST
Monica Riffe

⌄

secrets, and symbols. Here, the artist glued sections of sturdy, unprimed canvas to the pages of an elongated spiral-bound book and combined unexpected choices of colors, images, and offbeat found objects to tell a mysterious, exotic tale. The journal entry suggests a known world—represented by the old linen postcard—as well as an unknown world, where even the most mundane object (a sheet of loose-leaf paper reinforcements, for example) can appear to have deeper implications. Remnants from library books, office supplies, rubber stamps, and hole-punched tags add to the mystery, while watery drips of acrylic paint and blended colors create the look of an ancient archaeological text.

Try This: Infuse your pages with mystery and innovation by including unexpected and surprising combinations of collage elements. Overpaint with acrylics or gesso (or both!) to bury your collage elements. Then sand the surface of your pages, giving the various colors and textures a timeworn, frescolike surface. Use baby wipes—a surprisingly effective tool—for blending paints on a surface and for creating cloudlike effects.

"Art must take reality by surprise." —Francoise Sagan

P is for pockets,

patriotism, paints, and [tooth]picks. The expressive, flag-themed pages of this book are a result of exuberant fold-outs, clever add-ons, denim and paper pockets, and hidden enclosures. Constructed on a warm July day, the pages allow the viewer to slowly unfold and explore a festive parade of patriotic images, including song lyrics, a music CD, and a booklet of flag-themed postage stamps. The straight-from-the-heart emotion of these pages is underscored by thrifty dime-store purchases such as cardboard stencils (both the positive and negative versions of each letter), acrylic paints, classroom supplies, metal grommets and brads, and flag-themed toothpicks.

ARTIST
Michelle Ward

∧

Try This: Bring a sense of childlike exuberance to your altered books or art journals by using bargain-store finds such as poker chips, safety pins, pipe cleaners, felt, drink umbrellas, playing cards, adhesive stars, and notary stickers. Your surprising choices will bring a sense of play to your pages and will remind you of the joy of simple pleasures.

B is for buckle

ARTIST
Michelle Ward

∧

and for bringing home the memories of childhood rhymes and games. Creating pages in an art journal or altered book is a great way of reliving and redefining childhood remembrances, while expressing a current love for a wide variety of art supplies and materials. Notice how the orderly design of the pages underscores the rhythm of counting games, while the strong mix of touchable surfaces provides a sense of play and exploration. By pairing several contrasting textures, such as rugged canvas measuring tape, soft vintage ribbon, metal screening, brass stencils, and small pearlized buckles, the artist assures that the viewer will be treated to a series of visual reminders, far beyond "one, two, buckle my shoe."

is for envelope

ARTIST
Lynne Perrella
⌄

and for using everything in the studio. Large, rugged mailing envelopes are an excellent surface for doing all types of mixed-media artwork, including toner transfers, stamping, collage, and monoprinting. The artist used all of these techniques on a 9" × 12" (23 × 30 cm) envelope that was then cut in half and glued into the journal.

Try This: Carefully trim an unmounted alphabet stamp set and imprint the letters using acrylic paints. A paintbrush or makeup sponge is a good tool for applying paint. For a more impromptu effect, try dipping the stamp right onto the paint palette and make an imprint with several colors at once. Be sure to clean your stamps after using acrylic paints.

Or, try using ink pads in a more experimental way. Make multiple imprints, building up an accumulated series of colors for a more layered appearance. Warning: This technique will not appeal to those artists who like to keep their ink pads pristine!

 I is for interesting inserts.

The rugged black pages of this spiral-bound journal provide a perfect backdrop for the predominantly neutral tones of the pockets and insertions on this journal spread. Traditional office supplies, such as these hardworking library pockets, will stand up to unlimited painting, stamping, and applications of mixed-media supplies. In this instance, the artist used random applications of natural beeswax to add rich coloration and a smooth tactile surface to each pocket. (Wax can be safely heated in a crockpot [designated strictly for art purposes, please!] and applied with a soft bristle brush.) Her collections of alphabet-themed stamps came in handy, not only to label each pocket, but to imprint an enclosed shipping tag, tied with natural fibers, to illuminate each letter. When a tag is removed, the viewer is treated to a visual image and fascinating encyclopedia and dictionary entries on the flip side. (See examples at right.)

ARTIST
Lisa Renner

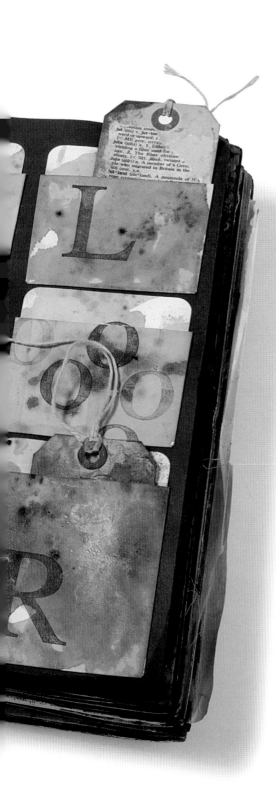

is for red rickrack

ARTIST
Claudine
Hellmuth
∨

and for revisiting another era. This artist has created a strong sense of nostalgia by using vintage textiles, combined with softened weathered ephemera, plus painted canvas surfaces that look anything but new. A carefully chosen color palette, plus recurring motifs of five-pointed stars, awning stripes, mattress ticking, and lines of stitching set the mood. Even the stenciled alphabet letters, A through G, with their serif style, refer to an earlier time. A canvas insert, trimmed in red rick-rack, features a painting of a horse and invites the viewer to make up a tale to complete the storybook nature of the pages.

The Telling Detail

The old adage, "Show 'em, don't tell 'em," is at play here. The artist selected colors, patterns, and images in order to evoke an earlier era. By leaving out words or specific details, she encourages the viewer to provide a story to accompany the artwork. What thoughts come to mind when you look at the painting of the horse, the rickrack, and the mattress fabric?

enjoy   laughter   delight

  is for
friendship.

ARTIST
Lesley Riley

∧

This artist made a special, behind-the-scenes effort to obtain a childhood photo of the artist who began this journal. She knew it would provide a surprise to the artist when the book finally returned home, as well as provoke strong memories. The mostly fabric page is full of touchable elements, including imprinted twill tape, a small leather heart, and a filigree "crown" that adorns the center portrait.

The Telling Detail

Both of these journals demonstrate how direct, heartfelt emotions can be conveyed through skillful choices in imagery, texture, and strong composition. Don't forget that simple materials can be used to tell powerful stories.

S is for sing, soar,

ARTIST
Lesley Jacobs
∧

and swoop. So many tactile details are presented on these skillful pages, and the artist has orchestrated all of them with care for a harmonious composition. The background is a combination of handmade papers, colored tissue paper, and joss paper. The artist builds on the cheerful outdoorsy feeling by imprinting the pages with a host of stamped words, adding wit and more color to the pages. In an homage to the ancient art of Asian stencils, the artist used a craft knife and black craft paper to cut out the central motifs of branches, flowers, and a lovely soaring bird. Other birds were carefully trimmed from an old print and added to the composition. As a finishing touch, imprints of Asian signature "chops" were added to the lower corner. These carefully crafted pages convey a feeling of exuberance, joy, and great style; a perfect blend of East and West.

T is for tea

of all kinds. Aside from the patience needed to create skillful silhouettes from black paper (see both journals on this spread) this artist brings a strong sense of design to everything she does. With an unerring ability to decide what to leave in, and what to leave out, the silhouette of a steaming tea pot sets the tone for a journal spread that evokes the joys of a restful, restorative cup. Flavors of tea, A through Z, are imprinted with rubber stamp alphabets of various sizes, and a childhood photo of an outdoor tea party assures a personal touch.

ARTIST
Lesley Jacobs
˅

Try This: "Chamomile, Irish Breakfast, Jasmine, Monkey King, Russian Caravan." This artistic listing of favorite teas provides a reminder that making lists is a wonderful way to get started with a journal page. Other possibilities? Listings of favorite books, films, songs, recipes, cities, and authors. Reserve some pages in your journal to enumerate your favorite things, and don't be surprised if your pages spill over to additional volumes. Why not devote an entire book to favorites?

is for kiosk

ARTIST
Sarah Fishburn
⌄

and for keeping alert for visual possibilities! Allow pure serendipity to provide fascinating, impossible-to-duplicate collage materials. Here, the artist discovered a heavily embellished kiosk plastered with numerous layers of old flyers, broadsides, and announcements. She peeled some of these from the outdoor surface to use in her mixed-media artwork. Other unexpected materials on these distinctive pages, including colorful drafting dots and text created with a label-making machine, come from an office-supply warehouse. The imprinted label strips provide the history of the kiosk papers and explain how they became part of the collaged pages in this journal.

Try This: Peeling papers from an outdoor kiosk is a great source for unexpected and unique collage materials. The next time you venture out for a typical run to the post office or grocery store, bring back three fascinating finds to use in your art journal, shadowboxes, or altered books. Let your imagination (and watchful eye) become tuned to new possibilities, and consider inviting a friend to join you for an art field trip.

B is for blocks

ARTIST
Monica Riffe

∧

and bandsaw! This artist envisioned a journal completely tiled with well-worn and well-loved alphabet blocks. To make this vision a reality, she began scouting around for the right materials and a method of trimming the blocks to make them suitable for a book cover. The artist used blocks from a stash of no-longer-needed toys in her children's room—a great example of finding everything right at hand. The next stop was the workshop, where she used a bandsaw to carefully trim the blocks to the proper thickness. The letters were then glued to a purchased journal, using contact cement. Edges of the cover were smudged with acrylic paints and brushed with beeswax, creating a book cover full of weathered charm.

Try This: A fun tip for aging alphabet blocks: Let children play with them! This artist has lots of ideas for adding well-worn character to almost any surface. She considers sandpaper a necessary staple on her art table and uses it when working with paper and wood. Try staining with diluted walnut crystals, tea, coffee, or a coating of beeswax— or a combination of all these ideas. Don't forget that rust and good old-fashioned dirt can be rubbed into a surface to make it look weathered and softly aged. Keith Lo Bue, a well-known assemblage artist, often lists "soil" as an important art material in his magnificent and highly coveted jewelry pieces.

O is for Our Lady

ARTIST
Lisa Hoffman
∨

of often-overlooked items of simple   beauty. There is nothing ordinary about this dimensional and artistically constructed journal page, although it is constructed of numerous throw-aways. An angelic postcard was the starting point, followed by a radiating corona of found objects, including natural reeds, tiny shells, a rusted metal disc, and a drain cover. Flexible wire and small invisible dots of diamond glaze dimensional adhesive combine to hold the construction together, and wax-encrusted cardstock frames the embellishment. These humble finds and ingenious inclusions create a stirring portrait; a perfect blend of heaven and earth.

Try This: Insert a piece of waxed paper behind your working page to protect the following pages from accidents. Weigh down your finished page overnight with a bag of rice to gently secure the surface. Insert a piece of bubble wrap, cut to size, into the journal to protect artwork during shipping.

And This: Achieve a rough and rustic look by using rusted craft wire. Keep a watchful eye for lightweight rusted wire at flea markets, but remember that real rusted wire will usually bleed onto any surface it touches—good or bad news, depending on the effect you want to achieve.

S is for stencils,

ARTIST
Linn C. Jacobs

∧

sunshine, and shadow. This artist decided to "hang a quilt on the line" without ever taking a stitch. She evokes the dark graphic designs of Amish crafters by blending deep shades of eggplant, maroon, olive, and raspberry patterned papers, served up with a rich dollop of black. Although vintage portraits play a central role, skillful blending and balancing of colors unites these pages as a strong composition. Two stenciled words, "True" and "Love," occupy the corners like eager square dancers, ready to promenade. Fabric swatches, glued into place, add to the finely crafted feeling of these moody and evocative pages.

M is for meeting

ARTIST
Lisa Hoffman

<

of minds, and meditation. The artist began these austere, cloudlike pages by applying handmade paper with matte medium, allowing it to fall into creases and folds. She then added acrylic paints to emphasize a watery, dreamlike mood. Fabric transfers on soft burlap provide the main visual elements for both pages, and the moods of simplicity and humanity are furthered by delicate add-ons of natural reeds, tiny sprigs of paper foliage, a crimped piece of imprinted tin, and a significant scarab. Reminiscent of heartfelt prayer flags, the fabric elements are bound to the slender reeds with wire, fibers, and soft ribbon ties.

D is for
definitions

ARTIST
Karen Michel
ʌ

and for dynamic color. Imagine a whole dictionary full of pages like these! Vivid colors, outlandishly large type, and alphabet letters that shout from the rooftops. All these surprising elements add an unexpected punch to a small pocket-sized journal. Rubber stamps, both purchased and hand-carved, allow the artist to imprint additional layers of information to the page, and her own handwriting on the wings of a butterfly provide an artful suggestion to "fly away home."

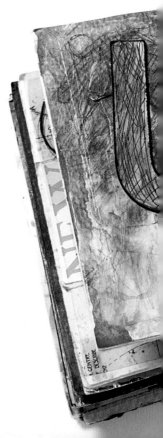

U is for unlimited

ARTIST
Shirley Ende-Saxe

⌄

layering. The small, detailed engravings that appear in dictionaries are a unique source of collage fodder. Combined with written definitions, rub-on letters, dimensional cardboard letters, and vivid mark-making, these traditional elements get a new graphic treatment in the hands of this artist. By using a variety of art supplies, including a fine-nibbed drafting pen, acrylic paints, and a soft graphite pencil, the artist created a fluid, tumbling pattern of color, pattern, and texture.

Try This: Look for old dictionaries at used book sales and library flea markets, and start a collection. Most children's dictionaries are full of interesting engravings and visual diagrams ready to use in collage. Old dictionaries often feature fascinating maps and topographic charts, plus gilded leather page tabs that can be removed and used in your own composition. Other good finds are medical dictionaries, atlases, and encyclopedias.

ARTIST
Lynne Perrella

B is for brainstorming.

Have you ever found yourself picking up a rusted, flattened bottle cap in a parking lot, and marveling at its patina, color, shape, or texture? To take the idea even further, have you made plans to incorporate it into a journal page or an assemblage? You can chastise yourself for being a magpie or a packrat, but you are merely spotting the keen possibilities in your surroundings.

Try This: To keep track of the truly tiny treats, keep them in a three-ring binder full of clear plastic slide pockets. When brainstorming a new project, look through the binder for a jumpstart. Each pocket may contain something that is engaging, unusual, strangely beautiful, or odd. Arranging and rearranging the objects in the pockets can become a favorite way to "warm up" while waiting for inspiration to hit.

"One of the secrets of a happy life is continuous small treats."

—Iris Murdoch

Word Play:
Text, Type, and Tales

3

We live in a world replete with competing and demanding messages from news organizations, PR firms, and advertisers attempting to command our undivided attention. While their carefully crafted communications entice and inform (or disinform), they lack the personal, vivid, and spontaneous quality of the pages in this chapter. When artists are asked why they create personal archives, such as visual journals, altered books, and one-of-a-kind artist books, a common answer emerges: "I want to create my own language." The artwork in this chapter will give you endless ideas about how to add words, text, inscribed marks, numerals, stenciled icons, and freewheeling messages to your artwork. Get ready to tell your own story.

One approach is to follow the impulse to inscribe your own words and musings across a page. These words, added to a visual page, colored background, or collaged surface, provide a defining touch of personal storytelling. Another approach is to search for passages and quotations that provide laser insight and deserve to be recorded. One of my favorite ways to begin a new page is to use a soft graphite pencil and write a favorite quote across the blank surface. Whether I choose to reintroduce the actual words to the completed page or not, the words help me to claim the page, get started, and have a focus for my artwork. The constant juggling of what to leave in, and what to leave out, is part of the joy of working with word play in books and collage. It's all about choices.

ARTIST
Lynne Perrella

T is for
too many.

ARTIST
Judi Riesch

But can you ever have too many? This artist used her entire collection of mostly antique brass stencils to create a handsome and substantial book cover, allowing other collections of tintypes and ephemera to show through the letter openings. She used contact cement to affix the stencils. A central window in the cover provides a sneak preview of the title page.

Try This: Working with multiples (of just about anything) is a wonderful approach to any of the mixed-media arts. Why use only one of your prized Australian matchbook covers, when you can tile the entire front of a special journal with the whole collection? Start thinking in terms of multiples, and review some of these suggestions for book cover embellishments:

- Wooden rulers or yard sticks
- Tiny vials and small glass bottles
- Vintage bone or ivory drapery rings
- Depression-era Bakelite buttons
- Game tiles, such as mah-jongg or anagrams
- Bottle caps, used as is or as frames for imagery
- Row-upon-row of brocade ribbons
- Vintage merit badges and honorary ribbons
- Snippets of old lace and trimmings
- Smaller-than-small wooden picture frames from a dollar store
- A collection of tin milagros, all sizes

T is for take twelve.

ARTIST
Judi Riesch
∧

Look closely. See if you can find all of the 12s on these two collaged and painted pages. To begin, the artist selected a dozen school children from a larger vintage photo. Each child wears a painted tag with a numeral from an old, weathered document. A dozen pearlized buttons take center position of the page, while torn swatches of mattress ticking and shirt fabric continue the hand-sewn feeling. The opposing page features a watchful schoolmarm, who oversees the children through a photo mat window as the clock strikes noon.

Try This: Look through the various pages in this chapter and try to determine the artistic intent behind the artwork. Oftentimes, artists use experimental approaches and allow their work to develop as they try different options. Other artists like to gather all their materials ahead of time, create a master plan for their pages, and then execute. What's your favorite way to stir up new ideas and keep them flowing?

The Telling Detail

Where do ideas come from? Looking at these two journal pages, we can imagine all the different impulses that might have sparked these entries. Was it a memory of a twelve o'clock recess bell? Was it a love of using old photographs to tell new stories? Did the artist discover an old sewing basket at a flea market and decide to use the fabrics to add color and texture to a page? Is the face at the window meant to be wistful or watchful?

M is for more

ARTIST
Sarah Fishburn
∨

than the sum of my parts—an artist's manifesto. Sometimes a theme can open doors to personal soul-searching and expressive self-definition. In this case, the artist has used the overview of the alphabet to tell a story about herself as a "Women of Letters." Proving that there is nothing mundane about the daily newspaper, she has used it as the first layer of her pages. To create a backdrop of color and pattern, she used a classroom alphabet stencil and spray paint to add sizzling hot pink letters. She generated her own words on a word processor, printed them out, and added them, collage style. The perfect signature to these ultra-personal pages is a photo of the artist, looking zesty and zingy.

The Telling Detail

An excerpt from the artist's manifesto:
"I am MORE than the sum of my parts.
I am NEVER (well almost NEVER) speechless.
OH, the things I can tell you.
I am the POEMS I remember from childhood."

Try This: Using the alphabet as your prompt, treat yourself to the challenge of writing a personal manifesto. Try to do this once a month, and put your collected words into a handmade, just-for-you journal.

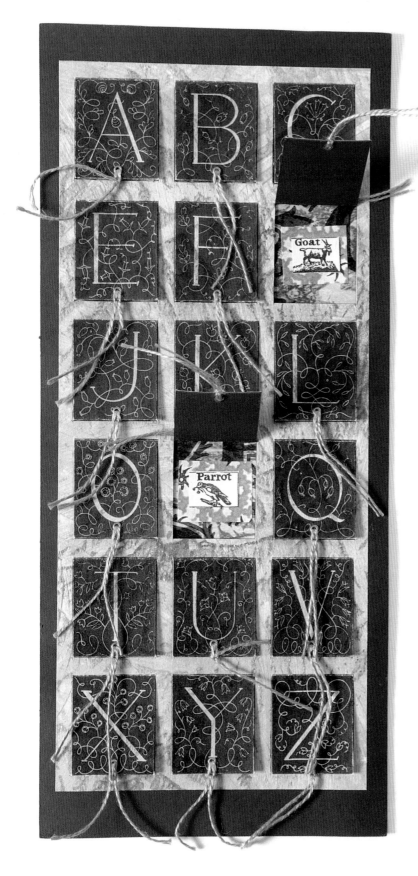

L is for lift,

and look. Stacked inside a decorated
hinged box, this journal consisted
of many separate pages created
using tactile elements. As the
box is explored, each unit can be
considered individually, making
the touchable aspect of this entry
even more appealing. The careful
construction allows the viewer to
lift each alphabet letter and peek
underneath, and the reward is a
wide range of colorful handmade
paste papers, plus a series of small
archival abecedary woodcut images.
The reference to childhood punch-
board games is obvious, and yet
the handsome selection of papers
and the careful construction and
design provide a sophisticated,
graphic mood.

ARTIST
Lesley Jacobs

<

 is for fibers,

and a fabulous face. Looking into her assortment of found objects, the artist was able to customize this sturdy and durable cover using a block of antique wooden type, vintage keys, die-cut letters, and a polymer clay impression from an antique doll. As a collector of faces, she has been known to take fist-sized balls of polymer clay along on her travels to make on-the-spot molds that are later transformed using faux/ancient painting techniques. The cascading tail of twisted fibers, yarns, metallic ribbons, and beads provides the perfect contrast to the rugged leather binding.

ARTIST
Lisa Renner

⋀

Try This: Borrow some of this artist's ideas for turning an already-wonderful purchased journal into something truly spectacular.

She suggests creating small *nichos* by working with tiny mint tins, holding them over a flame or using a heat gun to darken the surface. Create an assemblage to place inside, or merely glue a selected image into place. Drill small holes and attach the metal embellishment with wire.

The lids of defunct cans of paint can be used as circular frames and backgrounds. Consider leaving them out in the elements to rust naturally, or use Modern Options or Jax products to hasten the process. Insert a special collage element, prized piece of costume jewelry, nugget of beach glass, or smooth river stone. Use a Dremel to drill small holes around the perimeter, and weave fibers, leather strips, or string through the openings and attach the embellishment with wire.

Experiment with small picture frames from a dollar store by sanding or painting them. Keep in mind that the glass inserts can be replaced with nonbreakable Plexiglas or acetate transparencies. The frame, combined with surrounding design elements of leather, suede, or rugged handmade paper, could be a perfect customized cover embellishment. Also, you can invent a frame structure using short lengths of wooden tape measures, rulers, or yard sticks.

Use a jigsaw to cut out shapes from vintage game boards or old book covers. Newer game boards can be distressed with sandpaper for a weathered look, and a Dremel tool is useful for drilling small holes to attach the shapes with wire.

 N is for numbers

ARTIST
Lesley Jacobs
∧

game. How can you double the impact of a series of numbers skillfully cut from a black piece of paper using a craft knife? Use both the positive and the negative versions on opposing pages. The artist began creating the pages by pasting down large swatches of painted papers, giving the black numerals a vivid backdrop. The delicate, stylish design of the numbers provides a strong contrast to the urgent-looking painted brushstrokes.

W is for writing,

ARTIST
Teesha Moore
⌄

and getting it right. In this instance, the artist used a brush marker to cover a journal page with her own handwriting. A simple solution, yet the resulting marks were deeply personal and allowed her to save her thoughts about a moment, a day, a transition. This artist specializes in first creating the visual elements on her pages—here we see two collaged "fairies." She adds the written inscriptions on the run, when she has free time in an airport or coffee bar. Notice how her handwriting created an overall decorative pattern for the page, as well as a written account of one of those days.

Try This: Talk to most art journal devotees, and they will describe their continuing quest for the perfect marker. Since many journal pages are the outcome of numerous applications of art supplies, finding the perfect marker can be an inexact science, but be assured that there are countless possibilities. Both domestic and international manufacturers have flooded the market with markers that will write on almost any surface, in opaque, metallic, neon, and airbrushed effects. Bring your journal the next time you go marker shopping!

H is for humor.

ARTIST
Claudine
Hellmuth
ˇ

This artist makes us laugh about the omnipotent presence of facts and figures in our daily lives, while her tender line drawings remind us of the buoyancy of individuals. Deceptively simple art supplies, including strips of masking tape, white gesso, a fine-tipped writing pen, and minimalist collage elements combine to create a journal entry with a lighter side.

The Telling Detail

Notice how much mileage the artist gets out of a few minimal collage elements. She relies strongly on her own drawing style and painted areas of color to create the prevailing mood on the pages. Dramatic composition and feathery details illustrate that less really can be more.

is for color

ARTIST
Lynne Perrella
∧

and cardboard. This artist never passes up the opportunity to buy another packet of cardboard stencils. The sturdy, inexpensive stencils come in various sizes and can be used for monoprinting (as well as for their intended use.) Each heavily painted letter can also be glued down as a collage element. On these pages, a grouping of used stencils create a collaged composition. Additional drips, splatters, and random applications of acrylic paint unify the surface. The especially rugged paper of this blank journal set the stage for unlimited layering and applications of paint, and the unintentional beauty of the used stencils proves that recycling is always a good idea.

 F is for flapping,

fluttering flags. Art journals are a perfect place
to record our feelings and impressions about our
immediate surroundings. This artist celebrated the
opening day of boating season by creating these
multiple strands of artfully crafted flags. The individual
letters, in varying fonts, were generated with a word
processor, but the rest of the work was done by
hand, using strands of soft cotton thread, copper tape
(normally used in stained glass), and a strong variety
of patterned papers. She coated the pages with white
gesso, and used acrylic paints in a rainbow of colors
to create the vivid background. Each flag can be
lifted to discover a key word beneath: brilliant, lively,
zestful—words that easily describe the ingenious
construction of these colorful pages.

ARTIST
Lesley Jacobs

Try This: Craft stores and scrapbook emporiums are the perfect places to
find paper punches in every size and motif
imaginable. Paper punches are almost
as affordable as penny candy, and just as
addictive. For the heavier spenders and
truly devoted book artists, a complete set of
durable Japanese hole punches (in graduated
sizes) is a good investment. Hole punches,
as well as specialty craft scissors created the
multiple pennants on these pages and are
handy for endless projects. Start expanding
your tool collection!

"One purpose of art is to alert people to things they might have missed."

—Corita Kent

"Before linguistics, before the literal link
of language, there was listening."

—Hannah Merker

W is for words

ARTIST
Monica Riffe

of wisdom. There are hundreds of words on these two pages, but the ones that really matter are simple and dramatic: *speak* and *listen*. The artist makes an effective statement about communication, delivered by two large vivid faces, painted with acrylics. The painted shipping tags were stenciled with black paint, turning up the volume on the words and pressing the point. The entire background is filled with words gathered from magazines, junk mail, and newspapers, affixed with matte medium.

Try This: Go through a stack of magazines and harvest headlines and ad copy for your collage file. Don't forget foreign language publications for international flair.

P is for Players

Please Sign In. A sign-in page provides a place for notating all the artists who participated in the collaboration, and gives them yet another creative opportunity to register their contact information in the completed journal. This artist made use of an interoffice envelope, and glued it inside the back cover of her journal. A wide variety of pens, markers, stickers, faux postage, and rubber stamps have been used by the various artists to furnish the necessary information, while adding to the artful spirit of the completed journal.

ARTIST
Monica Riffe
∧

S is for sign in.

ARTIST
Lesley Jacobs
∨

This sign-in page is incorporated into the inside lid of a sturdy box. As each artist opened the enticing box, she discovered a shipping tag with lines provided for signatures and dates. A quick scan of the tag reveals that the box traveled for almost a year, picking up the perfect number of entries to fill it right to the top with artwork.

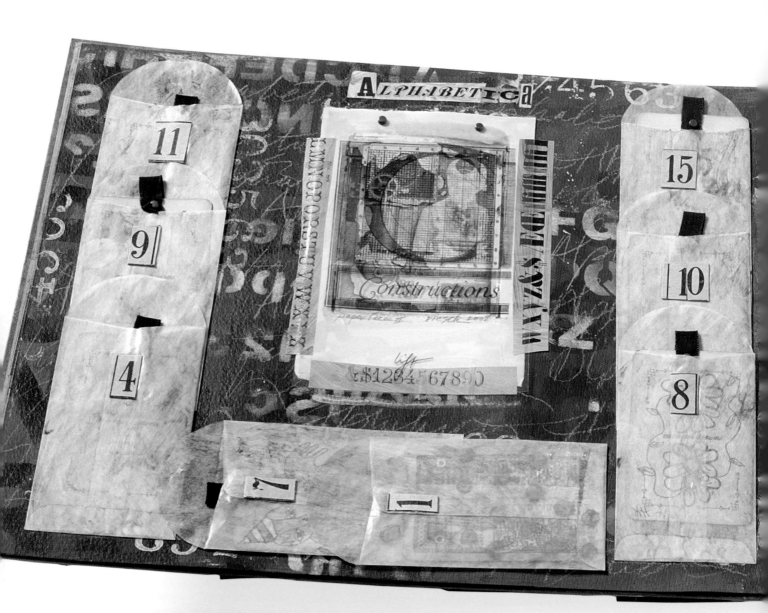

 W is for warm welcome.

This is an example of a sign-in page that continues the visual theme of the art journal. Vintage documents and rare books set the mood, and individual glassine envelopes contain an antique playing card for each participant to sign. A painted and stenciled background was created using dark acrylic paints. The artist included her Polaroid transfers with instructions to lift the imprinted transparencies. These two pages provide several interactive opportunities for the participating artists to decorate and sign the playing cards and to explore the various layers of the page.

ARTIST
Judi Riesch

The Telling Detail

When a collaborative journal has traveled throughout a routing list, and finally arrives home full of entries, it is cause for celebration. Usually these singular books are a reflection of months (and sometimes years) of creative participation by a group of respected peers. Most artists want to permanently document and archive who worked on their book, the dates that the work was done, and contact information for all participants. By setting aside a special place in the book for the artists to sign, the information becomes a meaningful part of the design of the book, while fulfilling the urge to get the facts straight. Notice how the artists in this chapter have enhanced the visual presentation of their books by including thematic sign-in pages. Collaborative journals are keepers, so make sure that your round-robin books include a place to notate the players.

P is for pincurls,

pixie haircuts, and pigtails. Here, childhood photos were added to a nostalgic sign-in page. Throughout this journal there were several opportunities for the artists to leave a school picture, tell about their favorite letter, or leave notes in a sturdy vintage book bag glued to the inside back cover. A firm reminder of grade school classroom workbooks, this journal provokes memories of another time and place.

ARTIST
Lesley Riley
∨

The Telling Detail

The artist incorporated her collection of early educational ephemera, including vintage primers, classroom aids, composition books, and spelling flashcards. Other artists added to the variety with inclusions such as old autograph books and schoolgirl fortune-telling games. As the journal made the rounds, the child in each artist emerged, and the resultant pages were full of remembrances and storytelling.

 is for map.

ARTIST
Shirley Ende-Saxe

^

The artist created the illusion of a mythic treasure map, allowing the viewer to fill in the details of the locale and the nature of the quest. The rich, textured surface relies on multiple applications of paint, collage elements, diary entries written with various writing implements, and cardboard stencils. The success of these pages comes from several different way of painting, including diluted washes, stenciled areas of solid colors, bold brush strokes, and a final application of watery drips.

Eye Candy:
Generating Images

4

> *"You must give birth to your images.*
> *They are the future waiting to be born."*
> —Rainer Maria Rilke

Where do ideas come from? *Everywhere.* Whether your ideas are sparked by common or uncommon sights, there are endless ways to translate everyday visual stimulation into exciting new works of art. Frequently, a successful mixed-media work results by blending unrelated images into a cohesive piece. The important thing is to be awake and aware of anything that might prompt the next great idea.

On any given day, we are surrounded by an endless stream of images. The fun begins when we realize that we can harness all this flotsam and jetsam for use in our artwork. Patterns, textures, colors, juxtapositions, reflections, tastes, music, and dialogue can be rummaged for their artistic potential and translated into new ideas. By skillfully observing our surroundings, we are able to constantly enliven our artistic approach.

It is comforting to remember that the next great idea is probably right around the corner. Maybe a reflection in a shop window, an image in a book, or a long-forgotten picture that triggers an avalanche of memories.

Most of the artists in this book are hunters and gatherers. They relish the fortuitous find, the "perfect something" that provides the ideal inspiration. Their studios overflow with images. Their collections may be stored in orderly flat files, jammed into drawers, pinned to bulletin boards, taped to the ceiling, haphazardly placed in sliding piles, or meticulously cataloged for instant access. But they have learned to trust their abilities to spot images with potential, and explore all the possibilities.

Once you surrender to the concept that no one else can observe and process the world exactly like you, you will be on your way to confidently crafting work that is original and distinctive. Look through the examples in this chapter and observe how the artists reinvent their chosen images, and breathe even more volume into them by working experimentally and with gusto.

ARTIST
Lynne Perrella

is for character count.

ARTIST
Lynne Perrella

While exploring the concept of the twenty-six letters of the alphabet, the artist gathered twenty-six antique portraits of long-lost characters and brought the photos up-to-date with applications of strong color straight from the brush, as well as monoprints, drips, and splatters. She added alphabet letters that were smeared with water-soluble oil pastels using press-on type from a stationery supply store. This artwork appeared on the cover of her journal, and she used the inside front cover to provide a key to all the characters, assigning them fictitious names from Abel to Zachariah.

The Telling Detail

Why resist the urge to buy that stack of vintage photos at an estate sale? Inexpensive and endlessly fascinating, old photographs and tintypes are a favorite studio essential for this artist. Whether remaining faithful to the vintage look, or disrupting the mood with applications of vivid color and "add-ons," such as collaged party hats, each image spurs a new idea. That alone is a good excuse to keep a box of old photos in the studio! Sort through them, take your pick, and make up names for the nearly forgotten folks. Copy them onto transparencies, dip them into wax, cut them apart, and reassemble in unlikely combinations. Specialize in categories like Mothers and Children, or maybe Weddings—or take all comers like this artist does. Sometimes an image asks to be used over and over, and making a file of photocopies is a good idea. Or, be fearless, and keep using your stacks of photos, knowing that a new old batch is waiting at the next flea market.

B is for boldness

ARTIST
Linn C. Jacobs

and "To be or not to be." The success of these bee-themed pages are the result of a contrast in scale and attitude of the design elements. The artist started with multiple layers of bold mark-making with acrylic paints, a large checkerboard stencil, and patterns made with a home decor faux-finishing tool. She added cardboard letter stencils, in both positive and negative versions, and a book-within-a-book surrounded by stamped bees with tactile liftable wings overlapping a significant quotation. With her confident use of color and pattern, this artist is able to weave a mood of flight and fancy, following her own stamped philosophy of "Faux Be It."

Try This: Take a leap! Are you inspired from a recent trip or vacation? Try creating a journal page or altered book based on the fascinating imprints and official markings that appear on passports, travel documents, and credentials. Cyanotypes are great for creating faux blueprints and surveys, or you might try to invent a personal map that charts your travels—real or imaginary.

Won't get... get a buzzing-noise like that. Just buzzing and buzzing without it's meaning something.

And the only reason for making a buzzing-noise that I know of is because you're a bee.

Winnie the Pooh

FAUX
BE IT

Q is for quirky,

and for taking your cue from odd photos. Half the fun of working with offbeat photographs is interpreting their story. Quite often, the colors or composition of an old photo is the doorway to creativity. Here, a row of white-garbed circus clowns hold their pose, awaiting the "poof!" of the flash powder. The addition of collaged letters suggests a retro circus broadside, and playful crayon marks result in a graphic and narrative look.

ARTIST
Teesha Moore
∨

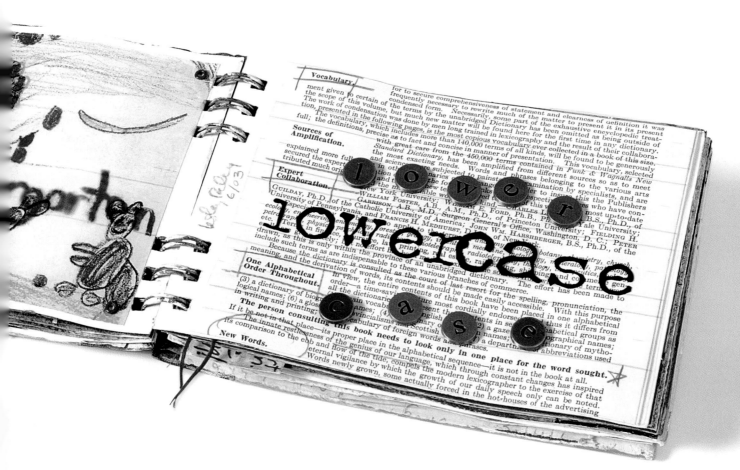

C is for crayons.

ARTIST
Lesley Riley

∧

It's hard to top the joyful exuberance of a child's crayon drawing, so why try to compete? You might find the perfect example on the refrigerator door, or maybe in your personal archives preserved by a doting Mom. Either way, consider using them as journal entries to recapture that youthful verve. This artist included a kindergarten drawing along with a childhood self-portrait, and balanced the colorful page with a quiet composition that is all words.

*"The core of creation is to summon an image
and the power to work with that image."*

—Anaïs Nin, "The Novel of the Future"

 **A** is for abstract.

This artist's confident approach to color, pattern, and layering has allowed her to make up her own distinctive visual language, using abstract shapes and forms to provide a background for writing and stitchery. Notice how the knots of sturdy thread add to the composition and provide yet another form of mark-making. Although this page incorporates a number of disparate elements including dictionary entries, alphabet stamp imprints, drawing, and handwriting, the overall design is cohesive, sophisticated, and distinctive.

ARTIST
Shirley Ende-Saxe
∧

is for home

ARTIST
Michelle Ward
∨

base and hand-carved stamps. When the artist first learned how to carve her own stamps, her biggest challenge was to know when to stop. Several sets of complete alphabets, in various sizes, were followed by a handsome set of large numerals. She began these pages by applying gesso, followed by successive layers of acrylic painting and mono-printing. She imprinted the numeral stamps with paint, and overprinted to create a rich, textured surface. Although these pages are a reminder that letters and numbers form their own unique patterning and design, the real significance is revealed by an enclosure in a small coin envelope attached to the spiral binding. The artist has taken all the house numbers of the various places she has lived, and used them to underscore her message about transition and finding our way back home.

Try This: There is probably a manufactured rubber stamp for any subject imaginable. From lipstick imprints to passport cancellations to a complete lineup of ancient man from Paleolithic to Neanderthal; someone has designed and manufactured a rubber stamp for every possible scenario. However, sometimes artists want to take matters into their own hands, and hand carve their own images. Whether your carving skills are primitive or impressive, adding imprints of your own hand-carved stamps to your pages and mail art is a perfect way to express yourself. Carving a whole set of alphabet letters or numbers might seem daunting, but simpler shapes can be easily carved in minutes to fill an on-the-spot desire for a stamp. Also, don't forget to "impress yourself" by carving a distinctive signature chop in the style of Asian calligraphers.

 G is for girls, glasses,

ARTIST
Lynne Perrella

and getting it all down on paper. Sometimes a memory will lie dormant for years, just waiting to be decoded. This artist came across photos of herself and her mother and was prompted to turn the images into a visual essay on the subject of eye glasses. Toner copies of two photos are the focal point. She used the images in various sizes and added numerous applications of feathery, dry brushing with acrylic paints to create a layered, painterly page. Using a makeup sponge, she coated antique wooden-type letters in acrylic paints to imprint the headline. The final touches are random monoprints from every color on her palette, assuring a deeply layered look to support the strong memories and new insights elicited by the photos.

wear glasses

Our first grade class assignment, each morning, was to copy from the blackboard. Miss Gantner would write the News of the Day on the board, and we would copy in pencil on yellow-lined paper, creating our own daily "newspaper" of Johnston School. One morning the blackboard read: "Surprise! Lynne has new glasses." The headline, written in chalk, was a revelation. Suddenly, the dreaded glasses were something special and very Lynne-like. They added something to my particular piece of the mosaic.... I was now the tall, artistic girl, with glasses. I was finally able to take notice of the number of undeniably-feminine women around me who wore glasses. Foremost of all, my own mother. (The addition of glasses had certainly not impeded her feminine verve and sparkle, and I began to enjoy hearing people say "my, you're getting to look so much like your mother." Glasses help me to see my world and my place in it.... Getting more than my fair share of "passes" along the way.)

Try This: Use scale and repetition for graphic punch. Consider using one image in various sizes to tell your visual story. This artist always makes numerous photocopies of the image she is going to work with, and experiments with different ways of cropping the image and weaving it into the composition. Sometimes using only one image to tell your story can be a plus. Many artists, from Warhol to Rauschenberg, were masters of using repetitive images to create dramatic, skillful compositions.

"You think dark is just one color, but it ain't. There's five or six kinds of black. Some silly, some woolly. Some just empty. Some like fingers. And it don't stay still. It moves and changes from one kind of black to another. Saying something is pitch black is like saying something is green. What kind of green? Green like my bottles? Green like a grasshopper? Green like a cucumber, lettuce, or green like the sky is just before it breaks loose to storm? Well, night black is the same way. Might as well be a rainbow."
—Toni Morrison

is for color.

Seeing red. Or feeling blue. Color provides us with a bottomless, constantly evolving, and completely individual language. Far beyond a vocabulary made up of hues and tints, color is a rich and complex concept—one of our most powerful tools for storytelling and communication. Whether you are mixing your colors, or using them straight from the tube, remember that color is one of the most significant tools in your creative arsenal.

ARTIST
Lynne Perrella

Try This: As a studio exercise and brain teaser, gather small swatches, paint chips, found objects, and fibers and arrange them according to color. Play with these groupings and selections as a way to start a design. As I made my selections for each space on the overall grid, the endless possibilities for each individual color grouping seemed to beg for its own journal—a perfect example of how larger ideas are born from experimental beginnings.

S is for simplicity

ARTIST
Claudine Hellmuth
∧

itself. This journal entry, light as a feather, was created to fit inside a child's vintage lunchbox. It is nearly weightless, with soft, frayed edges of fabric, strips of masking tape, and rows of white sewing machine stitching. The gentle childlike mood of the lunchbox is carried forward by this artist, with her affinity for simple yet carefully chosen and artistically composed design elements. This quiet composition invites the viewer to lean in close, notice the small details, and walk away with memories of summer days.

**is for
open-hearted**

ARTIST
Karen Michel

>

sentiments. This artist used several of her
signature touches to create this colorful printlike
page: an imprint with a hand-carved stamp, inkjet
transfers, metal tape that has been embossed
and stained, and color photocopies of previous
journal pages. The inscription to "keep
your heart open" appears at the bottom
of a page that is alive with rich, dense
color and supported by the enduring icons
she selected for this heartfelt journal entry.

 **is for object**

ARTIST
Claudine Hellmuth

<

of affection. If you have ever coated a journal page
with white gesso as the base for endless successive
layers, you may want to consider the polar-opposite
approach. In this case, the artist used gesso, applied
to a black journal page, as a backdrop to her light-
hearted collage composition. Entries from foreign
textbooks, maps, and a minimal use of stencils and
penciled lines define the secret dynamic between
the two figures. The bold brushstrokes of white
paint provide a hint of the artist's enthusiasm as she
began her pages.

M is for moody blues.

ARTIST
Sarah Fishburn

^

By weaving paints, transparencies, and tactile touches into the pages, the artist creates a sense of sea spray and fresh shipboard breezes, bringing the viewer on an aquatic journey. Paper stars suggest that the heavens will point the way to a sweet sail. A favorite art supply—spray paint—and plastic stencils create the first layers of the pages; the artist-designed transparencies were attached using brads. Strips of burnish-down narrow black tape provide a counterpoint to the abstract moody colors, and the attached ribbon ties suggest vintage middy blouses, bathing costumes, and boardwalk strolls from another era.

B is for bird.

ARTIST
Linn C. Jacobs
∨

Art journals and altered books are perfect venues for expressing a lifelong love of nature. This artist takes us inside her appreciation for winged creatures and their fascinating names, even inviting us to lift the wings of the paper birds. After seeing how this artist creates her backgrounds using a makeup sponge to apply the acrylic paint, you won't overlook the potential of purchased stencils. Using alternate layers of large and small motifs on the page, she built up a surface with quick-drying paints. Metallic paints add to the luminosity of her pages, and support her selected quote: "hope is a thing with feathers."

Try This: Sequin scrim is one of this artist's favorite studio essentials. The wide metallic strips, left over after sequins have been removed, is a durable and versatile art supply. Consider using it to prep a page, by using a credit card to distribute a heavy application of gel medium through the holes. After this is thoroughly dry, successive layers of acrylic paints can be applied, and the circular patterns of the scrim can be revealed by sanding the surface. This artist also specializes in using both opaque and metallic paints to apply stenciled marks (such as dots and checkerboards) as a way of adding variety and depth to her pages.

BIRDS: Avocet BLACKBIRD BLUEBIRD Bittern Booby Brant CROW DUCK EGRET FINCH Goose HAWK IBIS Kingfisher Loon

MEADOWLARK NIG OWL PHOEBE QUAIL ROBIN SWALLOW THRUSH VIREO WREN YELLOW BREASTED CHAT

Guide to Transfer Techniques
Get Letter-Perfect Results, or Relish in Happy Accidents

Transfer techniques allow artists to enrich and modify their chosen images in creatively different ways. Transferred artwork displays the hand of the artist rather than merely a simple collage element.

Each transfer process has its own unique look. Some result in soft and delicate images, while others are rough and more spontaneous looking. As with any technique, practice makes perfect, but the best thing about transfers is the artistic, often imperfect, effect you will achieve. Burnishing time will vary, depending on the size of the image. Lift a corner to see if you need more burnishing. Lesley Riley gathered the artists' favorite transfer techniques, and presents them on these pages, along with some perfect examples of journal entries in which transfers play a starring role.

 C is for canvas,

ARTIST
Lisa Renner

clues, and clarity. This artist culled the small details of a childhood photo to help her develop these revealing journal pages. She recounted her memories of an ivory taffeta dress with green satin bows, a favorite bracelet, and a girlish closed-mouth smile meant to hide a missing front tooth. On the facing page, her two younger brothers look on, providing the cheering section. This artist is comfortable working with numerous techniques for transferring photos to canvas. Final touches include strong washes of vivid acrylic color, a touchable coating of beeswax, and a diary entry copied onto a transparency and affixed with metal eyelets.

Try This: It's impossible to look at these pages without being lured by the memories and recollections that provoked them. Gather a grouping of your own childhood photos and study the small telling details. Background details, such as a street sign or a vehicle parked at a curb, can often provide a strong sense of place and time. Your journal pages are a perfect platform for visual storytelling; choose a photo and let your written reflections provide a theme.

Water Transfer of Inkjet Print on Fabric

Print an inkjet image onto glossy photo paper. Lightly dampen your fabric with a fine mist of water. Hold the image upright and spray it with water two to three times to cover. Lay the image face-down and burnish for 8 to 15 seconds, more if the image is large.

ARTIST: **LESLEY RILEY**

Polaroid Transfer onto Paper

Take a Polaroid photo, or copy an image onto Polaroid peel-apart film. Peel the film apart 15 seconds after exposure. Place the negative face-down on the paper and apply gentle, even pressure to the back of the negative by hand or roller to ensure complete contact. Burnish for about 90 seconds, then gently peel away the negative in a smooth motion.

ARTIST: **JUDI RIESCH**

Solvent Transfer of Black and White Toner Copy on Paper

Place the image face-down onto your paper or fabric. Brush the back of the image with solvent (acetone, Citrasolve, xylene), and burnish 8 to 15 seconds. Be sure to work in a well-ventilated area.

ARTIST: **MICHELLE WARD**

Inkjet Transfer from Paper onto Fabric with Soft Gel Medium

Print an image onto matte photo multiproject paper. Evenly brush a soft gel medium onto your fabric and smooth the brushstrokes with your finger. Apply the medium to the image. Lay the paper ink side down onto your fabric and burnish for 20 seconds.

ARTIST: **LESLEY RILEY**

Gel Medium Transfer from Inkjet Transparency onto Paper

Print an image onto inkjet transparency. Evenly brush soft gel medium onto your paper and smooth out the brushstrokes with your finger. Place the transparency ink side down onto your paper and burnish for about 20 seconds.

ARTIST: **LESLEY RILEY**

Water Transfer of Inkjet Image onto Paper

Print an image onto glossy photo paper. Lightly dampen the paper with a fine mist of water. Hold the image upright and spray with a fine mist two to three times to cover it. Lay the image face-down onto the paper and burnish for 8 to15 seconds, more if the image is large.

ARTIST: **LESLEY RILEY**

More Transfer Techniques

 S is for spirited

ARTIST
Karen Michel

and sensuous color. These journal pages show the rewards of working experimentally with transfers, and accepting the happy accidents that occur. Not only has the artist transferred her own drawings of birds to the page, but she has also introduced photographic elements and dictionary entries that seem to float in a colorful wash across the surface. Her use of full-throttle color blends skillfully with the transferred images. See the following page for more favored techniques for inkjet transfers.

Matte Medium Transfer onto Fabric

Print an image onto inkjet transparency. Evenly brush matte medium onto your fabric and smooth out the brushstrokes with your finger. Place the transparency ink side down onto your fabric and burnish for about 20 seconds.

ARTIST: **LESLEY RILEY**

Gel Medium Inkjet Transfer from Copy Paper onto Paper

Make an inkjet copy of the image on paper. Apply a generous amount of regular gel medium to receiving paper. Lay the copy image side down onto your receiving paper. Burnish and let sit for 10 seconds, then remove the paper. Paper fibers may remain; gentry rub them off.

ARTIST: **KAREN MICHEL**

Solvent Transfer of Color Copy onto Paper

Place a color image face down onto your paper or fabric. Brush the back of the image with solvent (acetone, Citrasolve, xylene), and burnish for 20 seconds, or more if the image is large. Be sure to work in a well-ventilated area.

ARTIST: **MICHELLE WARD**

Packing Tape (or Contact Paper) Transfer from Inkjet Copy onto Paper

Apply clear packing tape over your image and burnish well. Soak the tape and copy in warm water until paper is saturated. Gently rub the paper to remove it from the tape. Dry.

ARTIST: **KAREN MICHEL**

Caulk Transfer onto Paper

Use a surface that can get fairly wet. Use a color or black-and-white toner copy. Apply clear Elmer's Squeeze 'N' Caulk to receiving surface. Lay the copy face down and burnish. Dry overnight, or with a heat gun. When image is dry, wet paper and begin to rub away, revealing transfer. If paper bloom appears after dry, rewet and continue to rub.

ARTIST: **CLAUDINE HELLMUTH**

Inkjet Transfer onto Paper with Soft Gel Medium

Print image onto matte photo multiproject paper. Brush soft gel medium onto the paper and smooth the brushstrokes with a finger. Apply medium to the image. Lay the image ink side down onto paper and burnish for about 10 seconds. Work quickly, as papers will tear if the medium dries.

ARTIST: **LESLEY RILEY**

The Masters:
Artists Workshops

5

> *"An invisible red thread connects those who are destined to meet, regardless of time, place or circumstance. The thread may stretch or tangle, but never break."*
>
> —ancient Chinese proverb

Have you ever wanted to look over the shoulder of an artist and learn her tricks, techniques, and trade secrets? This is your chance!

There is much more to art than mere technique. In this chapter, the artists share insight into their creative processes and the stories behind their pages. As an extra bonus, they reveal their favorite studio accoutrements and some of their personal and creative influences.

If you expect artists to be secretive and protective of their ideas and methods, the openness of this group may surprise you. One of the reasons that mixed-media attracts talented people from so many other realms—jewelers, quilters, graphic designers, fiber artists, book arts experts, and stampers—is because they all share a zeal for cross-pollination. An eagerness to try new things, rather than concentrate on honing traditional time-honored techniques, is a common thread among the artists featured in this book.

Artistic collaboration is a way to create a community. It offers the perfect opportunity to learn from other artists and stretch your boundaries. During the course of this collaboration, the artists created a continual parade of inventive artwork while bound together by miles and miles of that "invisible red thread."

ARTIST
Lynne Perrella

Workshop: Composition
with Claudine Hellmuth

"Don't worry about your originality. You couldn't get rid of it even if you wanted to. It will stick with you and show up for better or worse in spite of all you or anyone else can do."

—Robert Henri

On Composition:

We can't always identify our reasons for liking a particular work of art. We don't always know why it works. But, frequently, a strong composition conveys a contextual meaning, and holds the interest of the viewer.

Try observing works of art, and then make notes in a journal or notebook about what appeals to you. Are you captured by the imagery? When looking at the artwork, where do you look first? Note the use of color in both dominant and subdominant roles. The goal is to train yourself to notice and observe strong composition, and let those skills inform your own original artwork.

Try This:

Pull out one of your own works of art. Close your eyes for ten seconds and then look at the work, noticing where your eye is directed. Does the artwork have a focal point? Think about how you could revise the artwork to create a more dramatic composition. Perhaps by mixing large and small elements, or changing the colors? What mood do you want your work to convey? What message were you trying to send to your viewer? Record these observations in your notebook, and remember that evaluating your artwork will allow you to maintain a strong focus. Even the best artists continue to learn from themselves and others.

The Inspiration:

The season provided the reason for these pages, created on a September day. As I was looking through my piles of visual elements, I spotted an image of a woman with the words "dramatic in nature," as well as a swatch of burnt orange fabric. I decided to emphasize the image of the tree by repeating it on the back of the page.

☞CREATING THE WORK:

Using gel medium, the artist affixed a photocopy of a woman to the page, and added a trimmed piece of orange fabric to further define the figure. She added an image of a tree to the dress using acrylic paint and a handmade stencil. Fine lines from an ink pen provided the final touch. On the opposite side, the artist took advantage of the vertical page layout by creating an elongated design. She glued down a background of large typewritten letters, brushed on acrylic paint to soften the image, and then added the large red tree using a handmade cardboard stencil and paints. Sponging with paints provided an expressive look, and an ink pen was used for the final mark-making.

STUDIO ESSENTIALS

1. Dog/cat beds
2. Radio
3. Acrylic paints
4. Ink pens
5. Papers
6. Lint roller
7. Fabric
8. Handmade stencils
9. Old photos
10. Gel medium

INFLUENCES

1. Anne Lamott
2. Alexander Calder
3. Cecily Heller
4. Michael Dooley
5. Sylvia Plath
6. David Sedaris
7. Kerry Smith
8. Katherine Streeter
9. Anora Spence
10. Noche Christ

Workshop: Layering

with Lynne Perrella

On Layering:

There is no way to fake layering. The only way to achieve a rich accumulated surface is to build it up gradually, allowing your paints to dry between layers. It isn't as slow and laborious of a process as it sounds. Acrylic paints are fast drying and can be applied in various ways to achieve different effects. I do not consider myself a painter, but I do use many different techniques for applying paints. Brushing, sponging, scrubbing down the wet paint with a rag, dry-brushing—these techniques all produce great effects. I also like to add other techniques between the paint layers, such as scribbling with colored pencils or sanding the whole page with sandpaper. Then, I add more paint! Monoprinting with wedges of cardboard gives me the printlike look that I favor, and of course the paint-encrusted wedges can be applied as collage elements. I like to recycle failed works of art. This gives me the accumulated surface look that I like, plus it gives me a second chance to make the work come out right. How do I know when a layered page is done? Easy—when it is time to move onto the next page!

"The poet, they say, borrows nothing that is foreign or unfamiliar to himself. He takes back what was his to begin with—those things, precisely, in which he recognizes himself."

—Wallace Fowlie

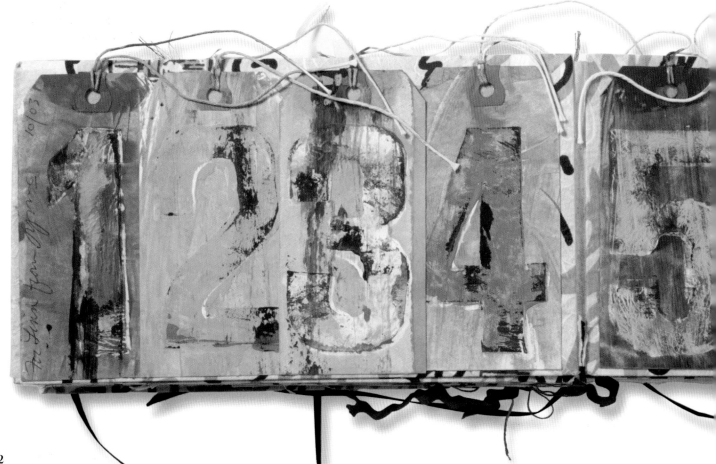

The Inspiration:

A respected artist sent me an impressive set of hand-carved numeral stamps, and I couldn't wait to use them. I loved their bold design and generous size. They reminded me of the lettering found on peeling outdoor broadsides, and I was eager to create that look using my favorite art supplies. I had a batch of large manila shipping tags on my desk that were just the right size for imprinting the numbers. Kismet! I had a whole stack of the painted tags on my drawing table when this accordion-fold journal arrived in the mail. The tags fit perfectly in a row across the pages.

➭CREATING THE WORK:

First the artist applied a light wash of acrylic paints to each tag. She made successive imprints with the stamps, gradually building up a collective surface of layers of acrylic colors. She worked experimentally, allowing the paints to dry between applications. Paints were applied in several ways including brush strokes, sponging with a cosmetic sponge, and dipping the stamp into the palette for a serendipitous look. She also dipped heavy cotton string into paints and allowed to harden. The completed tags were glued onto the book boards of the journal with heavy acrylic gel.

STUDIO ESSENTIALS

1. Acrylic paints
2. Sets of antique alphabet blocks
3. Countless books
4. Her studio shrine
5. White metal flat files
6. Paper, paper, and more paper
7. Constantly changing chaotic bulletin board
8. A 1962 AMI jukebox, full of 45 rpm records
9. Asian document boxes and suitcases
10. Toner copier

INFLUENCES

1. Hannelore Baron
2. Peter Beard
3. Romare Bearden
4. Sas Colby
5. Milton Glaser
6. Jack Kerouac
7. Norman Laliberte
8. Fred Otnes
9. Robert Rauschenberg
10. Melissa Zink

Workshop: Building Outward
with Lisa Hoffman

"Out beyond ideas of Right Doing and Wrong Doing,
there is a Field. I'll meet you there."

—Rumi

On Building Outward:

Adding twigs, pebbles, crushed bottle caps, and anything else that adds texture and dimension is a fantastic tool for self expression. The more I work, the more I am tempted to toss in the kitchen sink! For attachments, I favor using an awl, drill, or Dremel tool to make the holes. Always start with the smallest possible drill bit or needle. I use rusted craft wire for a rough and rustic look. Tempted to use just glue or adhesives to attach dimensional objects? It's risky. One of the most important things to remember when working dimensionally is to create a strong support for your artwork; otherwise it will rip the page, or hang forward. I favor working on lightweight mat board, and then attaching the finished artwork with YES Glue or 3L tape from Denmark. Use a bag of rice to weigh down a page overnight, and be sure to place a piece of wax paper behind your pages to prevent accidents. For gluing small stones or shells, I prefer Judi-Kins Diamond Glaze for a strong, invisible hold.

Try This:

Run a trail of this glue around the border of your page, and sprinkle it with finely crushed stone and iridescent glitter.

The Inspiration:

I used my relationship with the book's owner and what I know of her as my starting point. These pages reflect Linn's light, clear world view—like a wise, onlooking bird. The inserted flags describe Linn's various roles and my perception of her inner and outer beauty. Often I try to vary textures when layering to give the eye something to investigate, but in this case I kept the colors fairly consistent for an ethereal calm effect.

↬CREATING THE WORK:

The artist worked off book and started her entry with a piece of lightweight mat board. Layers of decorative papers and vellum were machine stitched using a large zigzag stitch and ball-point needle. A pocket was created by stitching additional layers of vellum, rigid screening brushed with a coating of acrylic paint, and woven paper with a tight weave. The title of the piece, "Linn Blossom," was generated on a word processor, imprinted on striped vellum, and attached with tiny silver brads. The removable "flags" were made from silk flowers on rigid stems, wrapped with ribbon. The artist trimmed out messages imprinted on vellum and machine stitched them to the flags. Two delicate, painted twigs, sanded and wrapped with twine and ribbon, and attached to the page with rusted wire provided the final touch.

LISA H. POST

STUDIO ESSENTIALS

1. My bulletin boards and walls of inspiration—visual paradise!
2. Shelf landscapes of junk and figurines for mixed media work
3. 8' × 2½' (2.4 × 0.8 m) work table hoisted up on PVC pipes—so all 5' 9" (1.8 m) of me can stand!
4. Separate sketch table for drawing
5. Pee-wee Herman plastic figures looking down over my work table
6. Old-fashioned paper cutter from a 1960s elementary school
7. Fireplace with Pinon pine logs from Santa Fe (it smells like incense!)
8. Big window that looks out on nature
9. Tall, skinny rubber stamp shelves and hundreds of stamps
10. A funky little bench with a statue of the Buddha, as well as beach glass, and softly worn river rocks.

INFLUENCES

1. Peter Max
2. Natalie Goldberg
3. Dan Eldon
4. Penny Sisto
5. Pablo Neruda
6. Simon Doonan
7. Jean-Piere Jeunet
8. The graphics department at Starbucks
9. Calef Brown
10. Danny Gregory

Workshop: Using Vintage Photos
with Judi Riesch

"*Creativity is not the finding of a thing, but the making something out of it after it is found.*"

—*James Russell Lowell*

On Using Vintage Photos:

Snapshots, cabinet cards, daguerreotypes, tintypes, as well as albums and frames, seem to find their way into most of the art I create. After years of hesitating to use the actual ephemera, I have started using the real thing more and more, to add a sense of authenticity and richness to my work. Photocopies are useful for some works of art, but overall I prefer to use actual photos, vintage papers, and documents. I enjoy discovering new ways to augment or change the photographs. I usually begin by cutting out the image, then adding paint and snippets of paper. Melted beeswax, brushed or dripped on, provides a translucent quality to the image. You can also try (carefully) dipping the entire photo into a crockpot full of wax. Next, try stamping, sanding, inscribing, or sponging onto the surface. Add anything that is on your drawing table, such as small bits of muslin, labels, and fibers. When trimming an old portrait, I always keep the surrounding area for future use. Not only is the negative space an interesting frame that can be used for future artwork, but the photographer's logos and typography make great collage elements. Vintage oval paper frames are also a favorite collectible of mine. I became interested in Polaroid transfers after taking a workshop, and the soft, sepialike quality of my transfers seem akin to the old photographs that I love to work with.

The Inspiration:

When Michelle's journal arrived, it contained a mini-CD full of songs about the number one. I was amused that one of my personal favorite songs, "One" from *A Chorus Line*, was not included, so that became my inspiration. Using a series of vintage dance photographs from the 1920s, I created a two-page spread with a trifold attachment. I wanted the dancers to look as though they had been drawn or painted on the pages, so I made photocopies and used paints, colored pencils, pastels, and crayons to add color and detail to the images.

☞CREATING THE WORK:

The artist prepped the pages with gesso, and added multiple layers of acrylic paints. Foam stamps dipped in paints created the harlequin-patterned background. The foldout was constructed from hot press print-making paper, and prepped in the same way as the book pages. Using photocopies of the various dance portraits, the artist trimmed out the figures and applied the prints to the pages using acrylic medium. She integrated the photo images into the page, using paints, pencils, and pastels. She added vintage ribbons and paper trims, and used eyelets to connect the trifold.

STUDIO ESSENTIALS

1. A nest of feather-covered papier-mâché eggs
2. A string of articulated tiny bisque dolls
3. Child's old tin lunch pail
4. Antique French laundry pins
5. An array of wooden santos and mannequins
6. Multiple glass domes
7. A mason jar filled with old silver baby spoons
8. Vintage leather jewelry boxes
9. Large stack of old marbled end pages
10. An assortment of old glass slides in my window

INFLUENCES

1. Eugene Atget
2. Merchant/Ivory
3. Joseph Cornell
4. Julia Margaret Cameron
5. Jules Cheret
6. Betty Friedan
7. Vivaldi
8. Berthe Morisot
9. Edith Wharton
10. John Riesch

Workshop: Attachments

with Lesley Jacobs

Working with Attachments:

I like to entice interaction and exploration with my page design. Elements that have to be touched, explored, or investigated provide mystery and give me yet another chance to communicate my message and captivate the viewer. Two sides of an item attached to a page provide two surfaces to work with. Attachments can be flaglike, lift up like windows, or dangle from a colorful silky thread, adding yet another element of texture and interest to the page. I also like to find ways of concealing an attachment, by enclosing it in another housing, envelope, or custom-designed holder. A booklet can provide a "book-within-a-book" element, and can be tied closed to entice the viewer into untying it for further investigation. When creating reinforcements, I try to use materials that are sturdy and durable, such as book cloth. I also like to use eyelets to reinforce small holes in paper that can fray and tear over time. Copper tape is one of my favorite materials. I use it to fortify edges that might curl or fray; plus, I like the shiny glint of the tape on my page. If including an envelope on your pages, try drawing the eye to it with something colorful—perhaps a tab or length of thread, and remember that the contents of the envelope may contain a story within the story. It's endless!

"You have your brush, you have your colors, you paint paradise, then in you go."

—Nikos Kazantakis

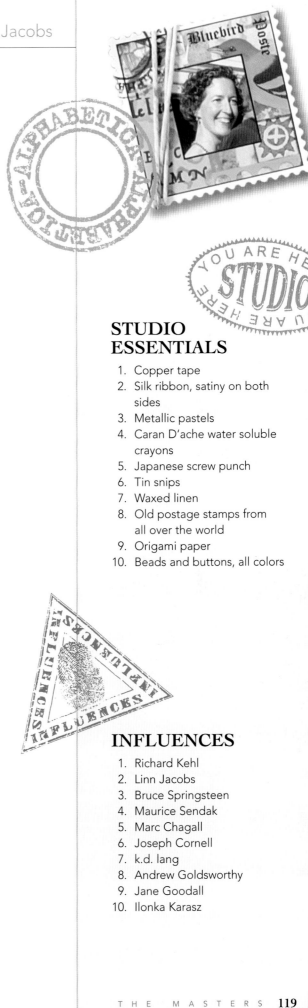

The Inspiration:

As I write this, I am aware of birds in the surrounding trees and a hummingbird nesting in my next-door neighbor's tree. The tiny moss and lichen nest is just big enough for the body of a bird. Birds make me think of color, the natural world, the mystery of an unidentified far-off song. When this journal arrived, I was fascinated that some of the artists had worked in it lengthwise, and others had created wide pages. I decided to use several diagonal "lifting" motifs and used my favorite bird theme for the nostalgic pages.

☞CREATING THE WORK:

The artist created a simple background, using paper with a fine metallic patterned motif as a backdrop. The dimensional heart-shaped attachments were collaged with papers, images of birds, tiny tags, and stamped words. The underside of each heart featured a letter and an appropriate quotation: "B = Belief," "C = Communication," and so on. Each heart was given an edging of gold paint, attached to the page with sturdy book cloth, and accented with leather hearts and copper tape.

STUDIO ESSENTIALS

1. Copper tape
2. Silk ribbon, satiny on both sides
3. Metallic pastels
4. Caran D'ache water soluble crayons
5. Japanese screw punch
6. Tin snips
7. Waxed linen
8. Old postage stamps from all over the world
9. Origami paper
10. Beads and buttons, all colors

INFLUENCES

1. Richard Kehl
2. Linn Jacobs
3. Bruce Springsteen
4. Maurice Sendak
5. Marc Chagall
6. Joseph Cornell
7. k.d. lang
8. Andrew Goldsworthy
9. Jane Goodall
10. Ilonka Karasz

Workshop: Transparencies
with Sarah Fishburn

"It is my misfortune—and probably my delight—to use things as my passions tell me. What a miserable fate for a painter who adores blondes to have to stop himself from putting them into a picture because they don't go with the basket of fruit! I put all the things I like into my pictures. The things—so much the worse for them. They just have to put up with it."

—Picasso

Working with Transparencies:

I have been experimenting with transparencies since 2000, and never get tired of the unending depth and singular quirkiness of the images. Whether I am using my own custom-designed transparencies, or using unprinted or preprinted (purchased) ones, I love using them for pages as well as pockets, envelopes, insertions, and enclosures. They can be buttoned, snapped, stapled, stitched, taped, or simply glued to a surface. I color my transparencies with acrylic paints, inks, lipstick, sharpies, and watercolor markers. Although transparencies can be used to transfer images, I feel their true value lies in their unique capability to allow us to add layer upon layer while maintaining the integrity of the view of each layer.

The Inspiration:

Knowing Claudine's penchant for working with spare, minimal compositions and soft vintage colors, I wanted to go in the opposite direction, and create something in her journal that had plenty of elements and a psychedelic color palette. Although, I admit that I did use some vintage photos and an actual old dishtowel to accomplish my pages. Voila!

⌦CREATING THE WORK:

The artist first applied a thin coating of spray paint. She also adhered tea-stained parchmentlike paper to both pages. She used her scanner and Photoshop to manipulate and colorize several of the page elements, including a 1960s-era dishtowel with butterfly motifs, vintage photos, and headlines. By using the Photoshop software to change and morph the colors of the motifs, and to create both positive and negative versions of each image, she was able to merge various layers and print out the collage on text-weight printer paper. She added some colored pencil markings, and attached printed transparencies with colorful brads for the final touch.

STUDIO ESSENTIALS

1. Art made by friends
2. Books, books, books
3. Buttons, ribbons, tulle
4. Peter Max pop art clock
5. Several boxes of Photoshop programs
6. Spray paint
7. Stencils
8. Various adhesive tapes
9. A retro Genie telephone
10. Many works in progress!

INFLUENCES

1. Adolphe-William Bouguereau
2. The Pre-Raphaelite movement
3. Marc Chagall
4. John Crowley
5. Mark Helprin
6. The 1960s
7. Leonard Cohen
8. Julie Christie
9. Luis Gonzalez Palma
10. Silver Gerety

Workshop: Using Great Quotes
with Linn C. Jacobs

"Sometimes with the bones of the black sticks left when the fire has gone out someone has written something in the ashes of your life. You are not leaving. You are arriving."

—David White

Working with Great Quotes:

I've written quotes on napkins, scraps of paper, my address book, notebooks, and the backs of envelopes. In short, whatever surface was available when I discovered the latest quotation. I've listed, stored, filed, and compiled memorable quotes over the years, and always try to keep track of the correct attribution. Once lost, these quotes are very hard to retrieve. I like to weave a quote into my artwork, letting the words inform the graphics, imagery, and colors used on the page. Words provide a kernel of an idea, and the inspirational flashpoint for what happens next. When I am sitting at my art table, I surround myself with a cornucopia of supplies that enable me to go in any direction. When inspiration strikes, I am ready!

The Inspiration:

Words themselves are revelations. I thought about Shirley who loves words and ideas, and then thought about color and quotes. Purple and green were my favorite colors to work with at that moment. Once started, it just grew. It came about in an organic fashion and gained its own momentum.

☞CREATING THE WORK:

The artist used acrylic paints, pastels, and rubber stamps to create the background. She then used a circular wooden Japanese game piece as a marking device to create a pattern. Her love of words and quotations led her to design pockets to contain special sentiments. A decorated tab was intended to draw the attention of the viewer and to invite her to take each card out of its pocket.

STUDIO ESSENTIALS

1. Coffee filters
2. Sequin scrim and stencils
3. Buttons
4. Embroidery thread
5. Paste papers
6. Colored pencils
7. Acrylic paints
8. Alphabet rubber stamps
9. Big sheet of glass on table top so it can be painted on, scraped off, without marring the tabletop
10. Envelopes of all sizes, hand made when necessary

INFLUENCES

1. Mary Oliver
2. Lesley Jacobs
3. Mae Sprenger
4. Hilah Conklin
5. Collette
6. Sas Colby
7. A. A. Milne
8. Bob Dylan
9. Rachel Carson
10. Lewis Carroll

Workshop: Faux and Ancient Surfaces *with Lisa Renner*

"With wings like feathered sails, she glides across the naked sky to horizon's gilded edge. Intoxicated, she balances on the precipice of divine enchantment, and with sweeping hand released, she paints the bronzed and purple dusk ... inhaling the mysteries of time, while exhaling heaven's stars."

—Lisa Renner

On Faux and Ancient Surfaces:

When I begin a new project, I usually have a vision of the finished result and this often dictates the supplies and materials that I gather to use. However, this vision is only a guideline and my real joy comes from the discovery process that occurs when I combine lots of art materials for an unexpected result. I begin with lots of seemingly unrelated products. For instance, if I am working on a background paper, I may get out spray dyes, acrylic paints, inks and glazes, walnut ink, chalks, metallic powders, watercolors, transparencies, stencils, image transfer materials, collage papers, rubber stamps, texture tools, and even encaustic wax! I may use all of these or just a few, but the goal is to work quickly and remain in the creative groove, rather than interrupt the flow to search for something. I love working with encaustic wax (both clear and colored), for its soft, touchable texture. While the wax is still hot, I often press rubber stamps into the surface to create a tactile surface. Rub N Buff is also a favorite, for adding highlights to wax. I never tire of the creative process, or the perpetual sense of discovery and surprise.

The Inspiration:

I know that Lynne likes color and texture, so I decided to create an entry in her journal that would explore those concepts, and personalize the pages by using the letters of her name. The use of letters went along with the theme of the collaboration, plus I decided to include interactive elements that could be removed from the clear pockets and viewed on both sides. I decided to experiment with some of Karen Michel's ideas about using bleach to alter photographs, and the journal entry took off from there!

☞CREATING THE WORK:

The artist created the background by applying a wash of acrylic paints to watercolor paper. Additional color was added with watercolor crayons, chalk, and imprints with alphabet stamps. She purchased clear vinyl at a fabric store, and created pockets to be attached with colored eyelets. The elements in the pockets were made from reject under-water vacation photos from a trip to Cancun, and the artist worked experimentally with bleach to achieve the unusual textures and effects.

She placed the photos on freezer paper, and put household bleach in a bowl and a spray bottle. Bleach was spooned onto some of the photos, and others were misted with the spray bottle. After a couple of minutes, the bleach altered the surface, creating bubbles, obliterating some colors, and completely changing others. The subject matter of the photos disappeared, and was replaced by wild and wonderful patterns. After rinsing off the photos, she patted them dry, and later added additional effects by scribbling with watercolor crayons, and rough sanding. The letters were cut out, and inserted into the pockets.

STUDIO ESSENTIALS

1. Books and magazines—art history, children's, bookbinding, polymer clay, doll making, ceramics, jewelry, home decor, and fashion.
2. Color copier
3. Images copied onto transparency film for image transfer and background papers
4. Old photographs and postcards
5. Antiquing aids: Jax products, Modern Options, walnut ink
6. Face molds, colored metallic powders, paints and glazes, miscellaneous paper pockets and tags, old pieces of jewelry, and fibers
7. Elfa shelving and bulletin boards to display artwork.
8. Large sheets of steel to rust paper
9. Big box of beads—glass, wood, ceramic, raku, seed, clay, all sizes and shapes
10. Miscellaneous drawers full of old hardware, keys, dominoes, game pieces, antique wooden letters, copper mesh, wire, metal tape

INFLUENCES

1. Tori Amos
2. Larry, Lauren & Nathan Renner
3. Dave McKean
4. Nick Bantock
5. Vincent Serbin
6. Jean Drysdale Green
7. Gustav Klimt
8. Tim Burton
9. Jean Dunnewold
10. Pablo Neruda

Workshop: Working with Fabric
with Lesley Riley

"Build yourself wings. Fly straight ahead. Walk a
straight line. Visit. Leave a special sign on the door.
Make a gift of words. Mark your path with books.
With clothes. With food. Join two distant places.
Two rocks. Two people. Bridge a river. Build a city
of sand. Raise up a mound."

—Milan Knizak

Working with Fabric:

Fabric is a forgiving medium. You can buy a little, or a lot. It has a texture that paper can never mimic. Loose fraying edges can dip and dangle seductively, adding a sense of movement. Fabric drinks up paint. You can stuff it, quilt it, gather, pleat, ruche, and fold it. Even store it in a haphazard way, wet it, tear it, dye it, paint or stamp on it, or crumble it up into a ball. Perfection is only a hot iron away. There is no paper that compares to the queen of fabrics: silk! It seduces me every time. I began using fabric in the usual way; making clothing and traditional quilts back in the 1960s and 1970s. Then, I began to treat it like any other art surface or medium, and it became my signature. It is both my canvas and my paint, my background and my focus. Any time I learn a new technique from a collage or paper artist, a jeweler or a printmaker, I instantly work to translate the information to fabric. I live in a mixed-media world, and my art and vision is colored by my passion for fabric.

The Inspiration:

The large pages of Lynne's journal really scared me, because I am used to working on much smaller surfaces. Although I doubted that I could design and fill such a big spread, as soon as I started adding fabrics to the mix, I felt inspired and at ease. Lynne reminds me of the wise woman archetype, gathering and inspiring friends and fellow artists with her wisdom and creativity. I thought the quote about the violets was a good metaphor for starting new projects and getting out of the comfort zone.

✐CREATING THE WORK:

The artist began by painting a brown paper bag with white gesso. She enlarged a favorite cabinet photo, and created an inkjet transfer with a transparency and soft gel medium. She crumbled the surface to add texture, then smoothed it out and added a wash of Golden Quinacridone fluid acrylic. The transfer was stitched to silk dupioni and collaged with embroidered silk and stamped green dupioni.

She created a large "W" in Photoshop, and printed it onto cotton duck through a laser printer. The cotton was stained and painted to match the transfer. Searching for a way to add dimensionality and surface interest to the page, the artist spied a folding ruler and mounted it over the cotton fabric with heavy duty adhesive. Completing the composition, and underlining the evocative quotation, a bunch of vintage velvet violets provided the final touch.

STUDIO ESSENTIALS

1. Golden Quinacridone Nickel Azo fluid acrylic
2. Off-white acrylic paint
3. Dupioni silk
4. Captivating images
5. Words of wisdom (quotes)
6. Adobe Photoshop
7. Computer
8. Transparencies
9. Golden matte medium
10. Sewing machine

INFLUENCES

1. Mozart
2. Mike Dooley
3. David Whyte
4. Nancy Slonin Aronie
5. Jean Ray Laury
6. Cecily Heller
7. Julia Margaret Cameron
8. May Sarton
9. Her father
10. Kelly Riley

Workshop: Building a Surface with Patterning *with Shirley Ende-Saxe*

"Well, you put down a color and
it calls for an answer, you have
to look at it like a melody."

—Romare Bearden

Working with Patterns:

Using pattern is a perfect way to exorcise the need for perfection. It is easy to apply, it is kinetic, and it gets way out of hand quickly! There is no way of telling when to quit a patterned page, so you might as well go overboard. I keep an art journal and work in it, without worrying about whether it is right or not. I make it a habit to be on guard against perfection and make plenty of messes, just to be sure that my art does not turn out deadly dull. Next to color, pattern is the most potent organizer of a surface. Repetition calls attention to itself. On this journal entry, the stripes and dots crowd next to each other and remain stationary. In other works, the dots remind me of birds in a flock, migrating across a page to a new destination. Vertical images supply needed balance and contrast.

The Inspiration:

Written journal entries say something, literally, and that is important to me, especially in a journal. But they also signify something, visually, that is more generic and mysterious. Any kind of writing implies meaning. It is the implication that visually interests me, a suggestion that there really is meaning and somebody out there understands it. Writing is both hopeful and revealing, whether the words are readable or not. Happily, it is also another form of pattern. Teesha's love of written journaling and use of pattern inspired me to create these pages.

☞CREATING THE WORK:

The artist favors beginning her pages with a layer of gesso; not only to create texture that will show through successive glazes, but to create a more complex ground of color. The following layer consisted of antique papers and dictionary entries. Clouds and other organic shapes are recurring images in this artist's work, and provide an interesting contrast to stripes and angles. Large spaces in the composition were reserved for writing, and acrylic paints were intentionally smeared to soften the look of the elements and introduce a sense of imperfection. She added dots with paint and fingertips, and cut up and adhered wildlife stamps before inscribing the final written entries.

STUDIO ESSENTIALS

1. Rocks
2. A squirrel skull
3. A variety of fused glass pieces
4. Piles of sea glass
5. A small wasp's nest
6. Baby doll head
7. Mail art
8. Postcards
9. Magazine pages stuck to the wall
10. Old books suitable for tearing up

INFLUENCES

1. Stephen J. Gould
2. Michael Pollen
3. Joseph Cornell
4. Romare Bearden
5. Joseph Campbell
6. Toni Morrison
7. Betye Saar
8. Maya Lin
9. Susan Sontag
10. Joyce Scott

Workshop: Metal Tape and Altered Images *with Karen Michel*

"We develop through experience. Therefore, hardships and misfortunes challenge us. It is in overcoming mistakes that we touch the song of life."

—Beatrice Wood

Working with Metal Tape:

Track down aluminum tape at your local hardware store. This tape is normally used for heating and air duct work. Because it is super-sticky and long pieces can be hard to control, be sure to work with short lengths of the tape. Once the tape is adhered to the surface, try burnishing it with a brayer to smooth out all seams. Or use metal imprinting stamps to hammer words into the surface. Stayz-On permanent ink pads work well for stamping. Freeform drawing and writing can be added to the tape with any tool that won't tear the surface. You can also try crinkling up the tape (with the wax paper backing still adhered) for an interesting textural effect. Experiment!

The Inspiration:

It was July 4th, and I was in my studio preparing to add my contribution to Lesley's great book. Inspired by the holiday and the people and concepts that this country was built on, I envisioned the letter "W." "We the Dreamers" reminds us that we build our realities from our dreams. Guided yet delicate, our dreams are dimensional and resilient.

☞ CREATING THE WORK:

The artist used aluminum ventilation tape (in plain as well as preprinted versions) found in hardware stores. She cut out small shapes and layered them on top of one another, using a tracing wheel from a sewing kit to add a riveted, quilted look. To add patina, she covered the entire surface with India ink, letting the ink set for about a minute, and then blotted the surface with a dry paper towel. She buffed the surface with a clean paper towel to get the desired finish, accenting the edges of the tape. On the reverse side, she painted the surface, and added the "W" card, as well as an inkjet image of the U. S. Constitution. Additional color was added with concentrated watercolors, and "WE" was stamped into the top corner. A piece of imprinted tissue paper, showing a hand-carved image, provided the final touch.

STUDIO ESSENTIALS

1. Children's art. My studio space is in a shared space so there is always lots of it around me.
2. My husband, Carlo—we work in the same studio.
3. Music, music, music.
4. Stacks of old books for altering and collage material
5. Well-worn work tables that can now be considered art!
6. Tons of artwork in progress.
7. Every type of black marker under the sun. The hunt for the perfect one continues…
8. Djembes, or African drums. My husband and I like to take breaks and let the rhythms fly!
9. We feed the pigeons that live behind our studio so there are always lots of birds.
10. The train! The train literally runs on top of our studio so there are a few rattles when the train goes by.

INFLUENCES

1. Pablo Neruda
2. Jack Kerouac
3. Frida Kahlo
4. Jean Michel Basquiat
5. Beatrice Wood
6. Crazy Horse
7. John Coltrane
8. Stevie Wonder
9. Bob Marley
10. Joseph Campbell

Workshop: Creating with
Recycled Papers *with Monica Riffe*

*"You have about ten minutes to act upon
an Idea before it slips into dreamland."*

—Buckminster Fuller

Creating with Recycled Papers:

"Trash coupage" is a term I made up for collages made from the detritus on my art table. Obviously, it is helpful to have lots of art fodder lying around. Not a problem! If I use a small portion of a piece of collage paper, I don't throw away the remainder. It will inevitably be used elsewhere. I keep scraps in baskets or color-coordinated bits in plastic bags on my work table. As I work, I rummage through the bags, looking for something that seems to speak to me. Often, I gesso a page before starting a collage, but I make sure to apply it in an uneven way. The paper will accept the paint in a different manner in the uncoated areas, and I like that effect. Also, if I am unhappy with the outcome of a work, I simply gesso over the whole thing and start again. The papers covered over by the gesso add a sedimentary layer of depth and interest to the overall piece. In fact, I frequently add papers as I apply layers of gesso to create a more textural base for my page.

The Inspiration:

My work table is usually a work of art in itself. Baskets, a flea market bowl, or vase made by a potter friend hold miscellaneous art fodder such as a marbled end page from an old book, an aerial photography map, a piece of netting, and dried rose petals. These elements can be pushed into gesso to become background texture, or added at a later stage to take on a more important presence in a finished piece. Having two sides to work with, I was able to use a subdued monochromatic look on one side of this journal entry, and revel in snappy color on the reverse. The vintage Cracker Jack prize was found during a flea market excursion with Sarah, so I enjoyed incorporating it into my pages in her lunchbox journal.

✎ CREATING THE WORK:

The artist used a brown file folder as the starting point of her page. She glued bits of found papers including a library card, a cigar box wrapper, French cheese wrap, a line from a Santa Fe travel brochure, a note, and a phone number. To attach papers she used YES glue, and for three-dimensional items such as buttons, charms, and a paintbrush she used Diamond Glaze dimensional adhesive. On the reverse side of the page, she began with a torn page from a stenography notebook, and imprinted the page with the poem "True Ephemera" by Tom Parsons.

STUDIO ESSENTIALS

1. Dried paint chips (I apply them with gel medium for "insta-color")
2. Sandpaper for aging images
3. Bottom of plastic fruit basket to sponge ink or paint through
4. Paper punches
5. Metal-working tools
6. Rusty tin, wire, charms, doodads, eyelets, beads, brads, bottle caps
7. Weathered clothes pins
8. Paper reinforcements
9. Rubber stamps and alphabets
10. Beeswax in a small crockpot

INFLUENCES

1. Leo Sewell
2. Nancy Anderson
3. Jane Dunnewold
4. Nick Bantock
5. Kaffe Fassett
6. Thomas Mann
7. Mexican folk art
8. Roberta and Dave Williamson
9. Bobby Hanson
10. Maira Kalman

Workshop: Constructions

with Michelle Ward

Working with Constructions:

My interest in creating clever means of extending a page, and going beyond a flat surface, probably comes from my curiosity about pop-up books. Foldouts, flaps, tuck-ins, or windows present platforms for involvement and interaction. When working in a visual journal or altered book, I often challenge myself to devise methods for achieving dimensional elements through construction on or within a page. Simple openings or windows can be cut with an X-Acto blade, and large decorative paper create openings that peer onto the next spread, prompting the viewer to turn the page. A piece of acetate, vellum, or mica can be mounted over an opening with eyelets, mini-brads, or even tape. If there isn't enough room in a journal to create a multipage spread, make an extension by attaching an extra panel of paper. Tie string, fibers, or decorative ribbon through punched holes in a panel. Affix foldouts with panels that open or cascade out. Try incorporating hidden messages into your pages. Mount envelopes of paper or glassine on a page, or attach them into the gutter or spiral binding of a journal. The envelopes can be host to any number of enclosures including decorated shipping tags, painted papers, secret notes, or even a mini-CD.

The Inspiration:

I have not met Linn in person, but her consistently cheerful disposition represents sunshine to me. I began working in her journal knowing I would incorporate images, song lyrics, and recordings of music with a sun theme. Inviting the viewer to be a participant in a page is an ongoing interest of mine.

☞CREATING THE WORK:

The artist coated the pages in acrylic paints, and created additional drop-down panels as platforms for imagery and text since the available portion left in this journal did not provide enough room for her entry. All panels were painted, and song lyrics were stamped and highlighted. She cut circular openings in both panels to allow the transparency overlay of the sun face to line up, when folded, over the mini-CD mounted onto the journal. The panels were attached with copper tape.

"One thing life has taught me: if you are interested, you never have to look for new interests. They come to you. When you are genuinely interested in one thing, it will always lead to something else."

—Eleanor Roosevelt

STUDIO ESSENTIALS

1. Signed copy of *The Humument*
2. Roll of chicken wire
3. Shelf of steeple clock cases
4. Assortment of printers type (Ms and Ws)
5. Two-hundred chess pieces
6. Five-hundred four-leaf clovers
7. Styrofoam wig heads
8. Collection of letter slots, door plates, and keyholes
9. Menagerie of Pierrots
10. A childhood dresser

INFLUENCES

1. Graham Ward
2. Julie Pearson
3. Zelda Fitzgerald
4. Augustus W. N. Pugin
5. Andreas Palladio
6. Charles Mackintosh
7. Sarah McLachlan
8. Louise Nevelson
9. Carolyn Quartermaine
10. Piero Fornasetti

Workshop: Working Intuitively
with Teesha Moore

"To vibrate, to accept, to expand. This is the new duty.
To give oneself as one is, to let life meet us as it really is,
to live for the moment and extract from each moment
all that it holds of truth, beauty and goodness...without
scruple, without vain questioning, in the spontaneous
desire of life, in childlike purity of heart. To be able to
be oneself, to dare to be happy and at last allow one's
soul to spread its wings."

—Jeanne de Vietinghoff

On Working Intuitively:

Don't agonize over the placement of every element on a page. Just allow the design to flow. I like to take a few moments to look at my page, and then act on the first inclination that comes to mind. By trusting the process of working intuitively, I am able to work quickly and use my creative impulses. I try to avoid getting bogged down with all the possibilities for a page, and try to tap into a personal energy source to let the artwork flow. Overthinking a piece is a sure way to lose the creative spark; let your soul, instead of your mind, take over a piece. By trusting your first instincts you will reap the added benefit of making art that is personal and from the heart.

Try This:

Get a piece of paper and crayons. Close your eyes. Start to draw. Trust that it will come out right. This is a great way of getting your mind out of your picture. After a few attempts, you will be surprised at the beautiful artwork that comes from this "inner knowing."

The Inspiration:

Our group was having an online discussion about cupcakes and recipes, and the subject inspired me to design these happy and spontaneous pages. I like to work with the first thing that comes to mind. Before I knew it, I started cutting shapes out of all the papers on my desk, including a magazine page showing a real cupcake. The longest part of the process was waiting for the watercolors to dry.

☞CREATING THE WORK:

Watercolor paints created the colorful background. The artist enjoyed working with an image of an actual cupcake, and then created her own exaggerated and colorful versions, using a wide variety of vivid papers (including scraps, wrapping paper, and wisps of text) for a horizontal lineup of repetitive and playful images. She used matte medium to affix the elements, and then began experimenting with ways of adding additional details and surface interest. Working quickly, the artist used various papers to add "cherries" to each design element. The real fun began when she spotted the possibility of using small faces to bring verve and personality to the joyous pages. In keeping with the alphabet theme of the collaboration, letters were added to each design element, and the artist reached for a nearby quotation dictionary to glean the perfect words to accompany the design. Swirls with a colorful crayon provided the final touch to a page full of energy, wit, and intuitive zeal.

STUDIO ESSENTIALS

1. Big pile of color copies from previous journal pages
2. One-inch (3 cm) paint brush, Daniel Smith watercolors, and Golden fluid acrylics
3. Caran D'ache neocolor II water soluble artist crayons. If I could have one thing to create with, this would be it.
4. Quote books and a dictionary
5. Scraps of fabric, ribbon, and trims in magnificent color combinations
6. Double-stick adhesive rollers with plenty of refills
7. Fluorescent pencils, gel pens, and highlighters
8. Glass pen and inks
9. Weird art dolls that sit and stare at me while I work
10. An iPod

INFLUENCES

1. Henrik Drescher
2. Saul Steinberg
3. Luc Besson
4. Barron Storey
5. David Mack
6. Susan Shie
7. Beth Piver
8. Guy Laliberte
9. Gil Bruvel
10. David & Diane Arkenstone

Contributing Artists

Artist Credits for *Alphabetica* Grid, pages 8, 9, and 11

A Lisa Renner
B Lynne Perrella
C Lisa Renner
D Lynne Perrella
E Lynne Perrella
F Lisa Hoffman
G Lynne Perrella
H Michelle Ward
I Lesley Jacobs
J Lisa Hoffman
K Shirley Ende-Saxe
L Judi Riesch

M Michelle Ward
N Lisa Hoffman
O Michelle Ward
P Lesley Jacobs
Q Judi Riesch
R Ma Vinci's Reliquary
S Judi Riesch
T Sarah Fishburn
U Lesley Jacobs
V Michelle Ward
W Claudine Hellmuth
X Lynne Perrella

Y Lynne Perrella
Z Lesley Riley
0 Lesley Riley
1 Lesley Riley
2 Lesley Riley
3 Lesley Riley
4 Lesley Riley
5 Lynne Perrella
6 Lesley Riley
7 Lesley Riley
8 Lesley Riley
9 Lesley Riley

Shirley Ende-Saxe
2306 North Haven Blvd.
Cuyahoga Falls, OH 44223-1559 USA
rgrace44223@yahoo.com

Sarah Fishburn
119 East Harvard St.
Fort Collins, CO 80525 USA
970-498-8996
sarah@sarahfishburn.com
www.sarahfishburn.com

Claudine Hellmuth
2457-A S. Hiawasse Rd., PMB #106
Orlando, FL 32835 USA
Chellmuth@aol.com
www.collageartist.com

Lisa Hoffman
Loveland, CO USA
970-669-6934
LisaHoffman@qwest.net

Lesley Jacobs
7728 18th Ave. NE
Seattle, WA 98115 USA
206-523-5255
lesleyj@earthlink.net

Linn C. Jacobs
Tacoma, WA 98403 USA

Karen Michel
karen@karenmichel.com
www.karenmichel.com

Teesha Moore
P.O. Box 3329
Renton, WA 98056 USA
artgirl777@aol.com
www.teeshamoore.com

Lynne Perrella
P. O. Box 194
Ancram, NY 12502 USA
www.LKPerrella.com

Lisa Renner
lisarenner@comcast.net

Judi Riesch
jjriesch@aol.com
www.itsmysite.com/judiriesch

Monica Riffe
Fort Collins, CO USA
monriffe@hotmail.com

Lesley Riley
7814 Hampden Ln.
Bethesda, MD 20814 USA
Lrileyart@aol.com
www.LaLasLand.com

Michelle Ward
P. O. Box 73
Piscataway, NJ 08855 USA
grnpep@optonline.net
www.greenpepperpress.com

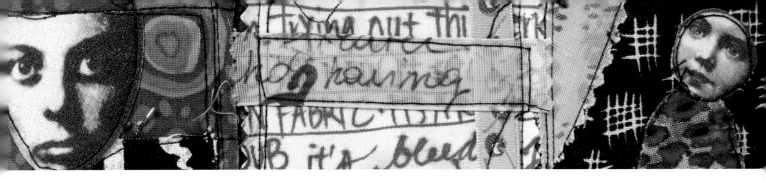

Resources

NORTH AMERICA

Alternative Arts Productions
P.O. Box 3329
Renton, WA 98056 USA
www.teeshamoore.com
*Rubber stamps, collage sheets,
publications, and more*

Anima Designs
5919 Verona Rd.
Verona, PA 15147 USA
www.animadesigns.com
*Rubber stamps, bookmaking supplies,
and ephemera*

Bonnie's Best Art Tools
3314 Inman Dr. NE
Atlanta, GA 30319 USA
www.coilconnection.com
*Coil binders, coils, eyelet punches,
book drills, and binding tools*

Coffee Break Designs
P. O. Box 34281
Indianapolis, IN 46234 USA
mikemeador@comcast.net
*Eyelets, embellishments, kits, and art
supplies*

Colophon Book Arts Supply
3611 Ryan St. SE
Lacey, WA 98503 USA
(360) 458-6920
*Mail-order bookbinding supplies,
decorative papers, and marbling
supplies*

Daniel Smith, Inc.
4150 First Ave. South
Seattle, WA 98134 USA
(206) 223-9599
www.danielsmith.com
Papers and art supplies

Dharma Trading Company
(800) 542-5227
www.dharmatrading.com
Textile craft supplies and wax

Dick Blick Art Materials
(800) 723-2787
www.dickblick.com
Mail order art and craft supplies

Fanciful's Inc.
1070 Leonard Rd.
Marathon, NY 13803 USA
(607) 849-6870
www.fancifulsinc.com
Charms and embellishments

Fiskars, Inc.
84th Ave. South
Wausau, WI 54401 USA
www.fiskars.com
Decorative punches and craft scissors

Green Pepper Press
P. O. Box 73
Piscataway, NJ 08855 USA
www.greenpepperpress.com
Unmounted rubber stamps, book kits

Harbor Freight
www.harborfreight.com
Aluminum foil tape, metal stamps

Hollander's
407 North Fifth St.
Ann Arbor, MI 48104 USA
(734) 741-7531
www.hollanders.com
*Decorative papers, bookbinding
supplies, book cloth*

Ichiyo Art Center
432 Paces Ferry Rd.
Atlanta, GA 30305 USA
(800) 535-2263
www.ichiyaart.com
*Japanese papers, origami supplies,
and rubber stamps*

Jacquard Products
P. O. Box 425
Healdsburg, CA 95448 USA
(800) 442-0455
*Paints, dyes, pigments, kits, and craft
accessories*

Light Impressions
(800) 828-6216
www.lightimpressions.com
*Archival photographic and scrapbook
supplies*

Ma Vinci's Reliquary
P. O. Box 472702
Aurora, CO 80047 USA
www.crafts.dm.net/mall/reliquary
Rubber stamp alphabet sets

Mantofev
www.mantofev.com
Ephemera, fabrics, and paper goods

Matthias Paper Corp.
301 Arlington Blvd.
Swedesboro, NJ 08085 USA
(800) 523-7633
Tyvek and other paper supplies

Michael's
www.michaels.com
Art and craft supplies

Modern Options
www.modernoptions.com
Crafting supplies

Paper and Ink Arts
3 North Second St.
Woodsboro, MD 21798 USA
(800) 736-7772
www.PaperinkArts.com
*Inks, pens, tools, books, and paper
for lettering and book artists*

Paper Source
www.paper-source.com
*Domestic and international decorative
and handmade papers; rubber stamps*

Pearl Paint Company
308 Canal St.
New York, NY 10013 USA
(800) 451-PEARL
Art and craft supplies

Plaid Enterprises, Inc.
3225 Westech Dr.
Norcross, GA 30092 USA
(800) 842-4197
*Acrylic paints, rubber stamps,
and craft supplies*

Portfolio Series Water-Soluble
  Oil Pastels
www.portfolioseries.com

Precious Metal Clay
3718 Cavalier Dr.
Garland, TX 75042 USA
(866) PMC-CLAY
www.pmcconnection.com
Clay and crafting supplies

Ranger Industries
Tinton Falls, NJ 07724 USA
(732) 389-3535
www.rangerink.com
*Ink pads, embossing supplies,
and crafting specialties*

Rugg Road Paper Company
105 Charles St.
Boston, MA 02114 USA
(617) 742-0002
*Handmade specialty papers,
and book arts*

Staedtler, Inc.
21900 Plummer St.
Chatsworth, CA 91311 USA
(818) 882-6000
www.staedtler-usa.com
*Paints, watercolor pencils, crayons,
brush markers, and pens*

Stampington & Company
www.stampington.com
*Rubber stamps, kits, crafting supplies,
and books*

Strathmore Artist Papers
www.strathmore.com
Papers and bookmaking supplies

Turtle Press
2215 Northwest Market St.
Seattle, WA 98107 USA
www.turtlearts.com
*Rubber stamp alphabet sets and
paper and book arts supplies*

Twinrocker Handmade Paper
100 East Third St.
Brookston, IN 47923 USA
(800) 757-8946
twinrocker@twinrocker.com

US Artquest, Inc.
(800) 200-7848
www.usartquest.com
*Perfect Paper Adhesive and art
and craft supplies*

INTERNATIONAL

Bondi Road Art Supplies
179-181 Bondi Rd.
Bondi, NSW 2026
Australia
+61 (02) 9387 3746
www.bondiroadart.com.au
Art and craft supplies

Collins Craft & School Supplies
Shop 2 / 199 Balcatta Rd.
Balcatta, WA 6021
Australia
+61 (08) 9345 3250
*Rubber stamps, inks, punches,
and crafting supplies*

Creative Crafts
11 The Square, Winchester
Hampshire WO23 9ES
UK
+44 01962 856266
www.creativecrafts.co.uk
Crafting supplies

Eckersley's Arts, Crafts and Imagination
Australia
+61 1800 227 116
www.eckersleys.com.au
Art and craft supplies

Graphigro
6e arrondisement
133, Rue De Rennes
Paris, France
www.graphigro.com
Art supplies

HobbyCraft
Stores throughout the UK
Head Office
Bournemouth, England
+44 01202 596100
www.hobbycraft.co.uk
Art and craft supplies

Japanese Paper Place
887 Queen St., W
Toronto ON M6J 1G5
Canada
(416) 703-0089
Japanese washi and decorative papers

John Lewis
Stores throughout the UK
Flagship Store
Oxford St.
London W1A 1EX
UK
+44 (0)207 629 7711
www.johnlewis.co.uk
Art and craft supplies

Keith Lo Bue
www.lobue-art.com
*Mixed-media assemblage, jewelry,
and workshops*

Paper-Ya
9-1666 Johnston St.
Vancouver, BC V6H 3S2
Canada
Handmade and specialty papers

Stampmania
Shop 2, 4 Newra Ln.
Newra, NSW 2541
Australia
www.stampmania.com.au
*Rubber stamps, inks, punches,
paints, and accessories*

Wills Quills
Shop 1, 166 Victoria Ave.
Chatswood, NSW 2067
Australia
+61 (02) 9411 2500
www.willsquills.com.au
*Exotic papers, bookbinding
accessories, and journals*

About the Author

Lynne Kendall Perrella is a mixed-media artist, author, designer, and workshop instructor. Her interests include collage, assemblage, one-of-a-kind books, and art journals. She conducts creativity workshops in the United States and abroad, and exhibits collage in galleries throughout the Berkshire Mountains. She is on the editorial advisory boards of *Somerset Studio* and *Legacy* magazines, and contributes frequent articles and artwork to various publications. Her work has appeared in several books, including *Collage for the Soul* (Quarry Books, 2003); *Altered Books, Collaborative Journals, and Other Adventures in Bookmaking* (Quarry Books, 2003); *Crafting Personal Shrines* (Lark Books, 2004); *True Colors, a Palette of Collaborative Art Journals* (Stampington & Company, 2003); *The Complete Guide to Altered Imagery* (Quarry Books, 2005); and *Quilted Memories* (Sterling/Chapelle, 2005), among others. She is the author of *Artists' Journals and Sketchbooks: Exploring and Creating Personal Pages* (Quarry Books, 2003). She lives with her husband, John, in Columbia County, New York.

www.LKPerrella.com

"You are lost the instant you know what the result will be."

—Juan Gris

Acknowledgments

This favorite quote reminds me that most creative ventures are about "living in the mess" and enjoying the often-chaotic journey. Thanks to the guiding hand of my editor, Mary Ann Hall, the process of bringing the *Alphabetica* collaboration to print was a joyous, stress-free caravan.

This book is a reflection of the respect, trust, and surrender that prevails among kindred artists. My thanks to all my *Alphabetica* co-conspirators:

Claudine, Judi, Karen, Lesley J, Lesley R, Lisa H, Lisa R, Michelle, Monica, Sarah, Shirley, and Teesha.

This book is lovingly dedicated to our dear friend and colleague, Linn C. Jacobs.

—Lynne Perrella

Linn C. Jacobs